CEO

The low-down on the top job

Kevin Kelly

FT Prentice Hall
FINANCIAL TIMES

An imprint of **Pearson Education**

Harlow, England • London • New York • Boston • San Francisco • Toronto • Sydney • Singapore • Hong Kong
Tokyo • Seoul • Taipei • New Delhi • Cape Town • Madrid • Mexico City • Amsterdam • Munich • Paris • Milan

Pearson Education Limited

Edinburgh Gate
Harlow CM20 2JE
Tel: +44 (0)1279 623623
Fax: +44 (0)1279 431059
Website: www.pearsoned.co.uk

First published in Great Britain in 2008

ISBN: 978-0-273-71353-1

British Library Cataloguing-in-Publication Data
A catalogue record for this book is available from the British Library

Library of Congress Cataloging-in-Publication Data
Kelly, Kevin.
    CEO : the low-down on the top job / Kevin Kelly.
        p. cm.
    Includes bibliographical references and index.
    ISBN 978-0-273-71353-1 (alk. paper)
  1. Chief executive officers. 2. Executives. 3.
Executive ability. I. Title.
    HD38.2.K466 2008
    658.4'2--dc22

2007038050

10 9 8 7 6 5 4 3 2
11 10 09 08

Typeset in 9.5/13pt in Din Regular by 30
Printed in Great Britain by Henry Ling Limited., at the Dorset Press, Dorchester, DT1 1HD.

The publisher's policy is to use paper manufactured from sustainable forests.

To my parents

Contents

Foreword

The World Economic Forum (WEF) is founded on the concept of bringing leaders – be they politicians, businessmen or social entrepreneurs together in a spirit of collaboration and dialogue.

Through the convening power of the Forum - whether via electronic platforms and multimedia participation or personal meetings - we seek to remedy some of the world's most intractable problems. Despite their varied backgrounds the leaders with whom we work share one common commitment – to improve the state of the world.

It is a long and difficult mission and one more endeavour for them to undertake in addition to their day-to-day responsibilities. I never underestimate how precious time is for each of these individuals. In *CEO* Kevin Kelly reminds us that it is not just how few hours there are in the day that preoccupies today's leaders. There are other key challenges and opportunities which unite these individuals – how to communicate so people understand, how to balance the needs of different interest groups, how to be a truly global leader and what it takes to leave a lasting legacy. Kevin has looked behind the headlines and the jargon to understand what the CEO role entails, physically, emotionally and politically. This is not a paint-by-numbers guide to becoming a CEO – I doubt such a book could exist, though many may make such a promise: it is instead an incisive study of what it takes to motivate people, and in doing so, what it means to be a leader in the 21st century.

Kevin and his colleagues at Heidrick & Struggles make it their business to understand the motivations, the strengths and weaknesses, and the 'fit' of established and aspiring executives. Kevin has many years of experience in executive search and could have written this book when he was a search consultant. But it would not have been the same piece of work. In taking on this project in the first year of his CEO role and reporting back from the front-line of leadership, Kevin has given us a perceptive insight into the constantly evolving position of the CEO. It is a dynamic and relevant account of a role which is so often referred to with generalities.

As Kevin mentions, as early as 1999 the World Economic Forum published a report which was presented at the Annual Meeting in Davos that explored the pressures incumbent on CEOs and the impact of taking on the `top job` to one's health, family and personal relationships.

Eight years on from that original report the world moves even faster and a CEO has only a very limited time to prove their worth. So, why do people do it? Kevin answers this question not just through his prose but with the tone of his entire book. From the moment *CEO* begins, the energy, motivation and excitement Kevin draws from his role is clearly apparent. This spirit - the real and human determination to make things better, resonates with the aspirations of the World Economic Forum, and defines the essence of contemporary global leadership today.

Professor Klaus Schwab, Founder and Executive Chairman of the World Economic Forum

Introduction

This book began with a question: 'What makes the right CEO?'

Working in executive search in Asia, in Europe and then in the United States this question has followed me from client meeting to client meeting, from country to country. And then in September 2006 I became a CEO myself.

It seemed the perfect time to actually set about finding an answer. What does make a successful CEO? What are their common skills? What are the expectations of CEOs? What are the pressures? How do they spend their days? As a relatively recently appointed CEO I know this book is unusual. Most CEOs get their faces on magazine covers and then write their memoirs after they have retired. These books have the benefit of hindsight but often end up being a weighty justification of past acts, or just a collection of anecdotes.

This book is different. I knew my early months as CEO would be very busy but I believe being a CEO is about learning as well as leading, and writing the book was a priority. As Stephen Miles, a partner in Leadership Consulting at Heidrick & Struggles, said to me, 'It's what you learn after you know everything that counts.' In my experience, most CEOs fail because they think they know everything. For me, what better time to learn about being a CEO than by sitting down and talking to my peers early on and hopefully saving us all some time?

The CEOs I have talked to are from all around the globe; some are seasoned leaders, others are new to the job, like me. But whatever their experience, common themes emerge. It doesn't matter which organization they're in – the people issues, the communication issues, the complexities of compensation, finding time for family – they're the same for each and every CEO. Many of these mirror my own preoccupations as CEO – those common dilemmas that come up every day.

The first is communication: how it can be misunderstood, and how it should be handled.

The second is compensation – not just in a monetary sense but also in working to make every employee feel valued so that they look forward to work each morning. Because really it all comes down to people, doesn't it? What is amazing to me is that we study business at university or business school and spend 95 per cent of the time learning about strategy, marketing, corporate finance, organizational structures etc., and about 5 per cent on people skills. Yet, when we finish our studies and start working we immediately find the opposite to be true – personnel issues fill our days, whether you're working in an organization of ten or ten thousand. Day to day, every plan you make and every strategy you devise revolves around having the right people in place.

Change is another preoccupation. Charles Darwin said: 'It is not the strongest of the species that survives, nor the most intelligent that survives. It is the one that is the most adaptable to change.' How you manage, direct and communicate change fascinates me. I remember speaking to a CEO in Germany, and he observed that whenever a leader talks about change, employees always expect the worst. How does a CEO direct change for the good of the organization and the people?

The final point that you will see me calling back to throughout this book is the most fundamental to me, that is, doing what's right versus doing what's popular. It sounds simple, but if I test my actions against this each day, then I know I can't have done a bad job.

I must admit, writing this book has been therapeutic. As a CEO you cannot talk freely about problems or what *might* be happening. What you say has an impact on employees, shareholders, investors and the media. You have to communicate with care. Writing this book provided me with an incentive to look at the CEO role with some long-term, long-distance perspective and to talk to people outside the organization about what the job actually means to them.

I hope *CEO* is as helpful to you as the writing of it has been to me.

Using this book

CEO is an exploration of the CEO's job, now and in the future. It is not a 'how to' book – if it was it would retail at several million dollars! But it is practically useful in that it surfaces and explores the key issues that CEOs have to deal with, from day one when they take the job to the end of their careers. CEOs, would-be CEOs and CEO-watchers (everyone else in the organization) can begin with the sections which most accurately mirror their situation and the issues they currently face.

Chapter 1 Getting there Every CEO is unique. Every journey to the corner office is different. But what do you really need to know about the route to the top job?

Chapter 2 My first 100 days There are many books about what CEOs should and should not do when they take over. One hundred days is only a short time, and far shorter when everyone inside the company and out is watching your every move. So, what does the new CEO need to do before taking the job and when the first day beckons?

Chapter 3 The job: leadership, strategy and execution The CEO's job begins with leadership. The CEO is in charge. But where are they leading their people and how can they ensure they get there? Without strategy and execution, leadership is decorative.

Chapter 4 The job: communication and people How do you convince people that you are the person to provide leadership, that your strategy is the right one and that execution relies on everyone contributing?

Chapter 5 The rise and rise of the global CEO Increasingly, a CEO's work takes place in a global arena. What does this really mean? If you're CEO of a tractor parts manufacturer in Deerpark, Ohio, what does the world matter?

Chapter 6 My board and I It is the moment of truth: the first board meeting. How does it work? You barely know the people around the table and they expect you to have delivered sterling results instantly. How can you manage your board?

Chapter 7 Me myself I You're under pressure from all sides – investors, your board, not to mention your people, unions, competitors . . . and more. How can you keep your sanity and live happily when you could – should? – be working and travelling 24/7?

Chapter 8 Trials, tribulations and triumphs What are the good things about the job? What are the worst?

Chapter 9 Tomorrow's CEOs What is the identikit of the CEO of 2020? What skills and capabilities do you need to develop if you are to make the golden career leap?

Chapter 10 The life beyond Nothing lasts for ever. Today's magazine-cover CEO superstar is tomorrow's corporate footnote. But how does this affect CEOs when they're in the job and how can they prepare for the life beyond?

L. Kevin Kelly
London, June 2007

Acknowledgements

I would like to thank all those leaders who found the time in their schedules to talk to me about the CEO's job. In particular, thanks are due to:

Jacques Aigrain, CEO, Swiss Re, Switzerland

Richard Baker, CEO, Alliance Boots, UK

Carlos Ghosn, President and CEO, Nissan, Japan, and President and CEO, Renault, France

Seung-Yu Kim, CEO, Hana Financial Group, Korea

Gary Knell, President and CEO, Sesame Workshop, United States

Bruno Lafont, Chairman and CEO, Lafarge, France

Chip McClure, Chairman, CEO and President, ArvinMeritor, United States

Takeshi Niinami, President and CEO, Lawson, Japan

Monika Ribar, President and CEO, Panalpina, Switzerland

Stuart Rose, CEO, Marks & Spencer, UK

Carl Schramm, President and CEO, Kaufmann Foundation, United States

H. Patrick Swygert, President of Howard University, United States

The Senior Chairman of Heidrick & Struggles, Gerry Roche, was also kind enough to lend me insights from his legendary career in search. Gerry has probably recruited more CEOs than anyone else in the world and I am very grateful for his time.

Steve Tappin of Heidrick & Struggles provided great comment on his own extensive research into CEOs in the UK.

My thanks to Heidrick & Struggles board members Richard Beattie (Simpson Thacher & Bartlett) and Jill Kanin-Lovers, who both offered invaluable assistance with the board chapter.

To Stuart Crainer without whom the writing of this book would not have been possible.

To my publisher Liz Gooster for all her enthusiasm and good advice, and to Narda Shirley and Tashi Lassalle for their inspiration and creative support in turning this book from an idea into a reality.

The support and hard work of Jacqueline Wilson and Claire Davies made this task a whole lot easier.

Thanks to David Peters for his eagle-eyed proofing.

Inhye Kim, Bernard Zen-Ruffinen, Grace Moon, Fran Minogue, Nathaniel J. Sutton and John Gardner for finding time to help me set up interviews with the CEOs. And Preeti Seshadri for her research help.

My wife Michele for her love, support and, most of all, her patience, particularly when it comes to replacing light bulbs.

To all my great colleagues at Heidrick & Struggles.

. . . and to my friend Sam.

A DAY IN THE LIFE OF A CEO

Tuesday, 15 May 2007

5.45 am	My wife is out of town. I get up and go for a run. I think while I run. Most CEOs I talk to do something like this, whether it's playing tennis or going to the gym.
	I then get my four kids up (8, 6, 4 and 2 years old) and dressed, me dressed, get them to the bus stop, me to the train station.
7.45 am	Call the Shanghai office to check in, scan through my emails on the train and then jump into cab and make calls until I arrive at the office at 8.15 when I have a 15 minute catch-up with my executive assistant.
8.30 am	Speak to our chief financial officer for Asia-Pacific who is based out of Sydney.
9.00 am	Talk to one of our UK-based consultants about the successes of a new private equity initiative we are working on in the firm.
9.30 am	Meeting with Human Resources about a couple of key new hires in Europe.
10.30 am	Preparation for upcoming board meeting with the director of communications.
11.30 am	Meeting with three of our top-billing consultants.
12.15 pm	Lunch with the head of the World Economic Forum, Klaus Schwab, to discuss a new joint initiative with Heidrick & Struggles.
1.30–2.30 pm	360-degree review with external coach/consultant as part of the work we're doing realigning our leadership team.
2.30 pm	Call our office managing partner in Paris.
3.00 pm	Squeeze in a meeting with a US consultant on a last-minute trip to the London office.
3.30 pm	Meeting to discuss strategic reorganization of our practices in North America.
4.30 pm	Meet with Stuart Rose, CEO of Marks & Spencer.
5.45 pm	Call to our CFO Eileen Kamerick.
6.00 pm	Call with the external consulting firm who are reviewing the Heidrick & Struggles business model.

▶

6.30 pm	Call with a partner in São Paolo and then another in Encino.
7.00 pm	Call company senior chairman Gerry Roche from a cab on the way to the station. Then more emails to check while I'm on the train.
8.00 pm	Get home and my daughter tells me she needs help with her homework on prisms. I have to eat my dinner, get the three younger children to bed and read their bedtime stories, and figure out what a prism is.
9.00–10.45 pm	Executive committee call.
10.46 pm	Head of Asia-Pacific calls asking for a couple of extra minutes – I say can we talk tomorrow morning? He says fine, sure, but still end up chatting.
	And suddenly it's 11.20 pm and I hit the pillow until the alarm goes off at 5.45 again.

People often ask me how I spend my time now I am a CEO. That was a pretty typical day when I worked from our London office (I relocated to Chicago in July 2007). The rest of the time I am on the road. The reality is that every time I am on the move, I make a call; every time I have a break I call someone. I go through a mental list of who I haven't spoken to for a while or someone who I know has a new piece of work on, or family news – they've just had a new baby or something.

Why do I tell you all this? Because the life of a CEO is not for everyone. It is a gruelling, stressful and often lonely, existence. I want you to know that up front, before you get involved or before you start dreaming of being a CEO. I want you to know that it is physically, mentally and emotionally demanding. And, of course, there is no guarantee of success or even survival in the post. So why do it? Because, on a good day, it is also the best job in the world.

Chapter **1**

Getting there

Every CEO is unique. Every journey to the corner office is different. But what do you really need to know about the route to the top job?

The ideal person to become the CEO is someone who has a successful and demonstrable record in doing and planning; someone who has a proven record with experience in running profit centres, staff support functions and, especially, the strategic planning function within a corporation. Now, if you have somebody that can strategize and execute and you've got a record that they have done it successfully, then you're home.

Gerry Roche, Senior Chairman, Heidrick & Struggles

Moments in time

There are moments in time, moments which change the course of events, which change entire organizations, alter the paths of careers, and shape lives. For corporations these critical, path-shaping moments are when a new CEO is appointed. Time stands still. The organization and its individuals are held up to blinding scrutiny. What they stand for, what they aspire to be and how they intend to get there are appraised from every angle.

The pressure is intense for those on the board, those charged with hiring and firing. Get it right and they are heroes. Look at Jim McNerney's appointment as chairman and CEO of 3M.

McNerney was fresh from the Jack Welch succession race at General Electric (GE), where he was beaten to the number 1 spot by Jeff Immelt. Having worked across a broad range of GE business units, and with extensive international experience, including two years running GE's Asian operations, he was considered a perfect fit with 3M.

Before the announcement, 3M's stock was languishing in the $80 to $90 range. On the day McNerney was hired the stock jumped from $99 to $105, reaching a 52-week high of $122 within a month. All because McNerney was seen as a great choice.

After a slight hiccup at the outset, referring to 3M as GE at his first shareholders' meeting, McNerney brought some GE management science to bear on the wildfire innovation culture of 3M, introducing Six Sigma, cutting overheads, and creating a leadership development institute along the lines of GE's Crotonville. At the same time, however, 3M's new CEO, the first outsider to lead the company, emphasized that, 'the story here is rejuvenation of a talented group of people, rather than replacement of a mediocre group of people'.

Between 1995 and 2000, shareholder returns at 3M had lagged behind the S&P 500. With McNerney at the helm, the shares climbed beyond the $120 mark while the S&P 500 dipped by 30 per cent.

No wonder, then, that Boeing's shares leapt 7 per cent ($3.9 billion) and 3M's slumped 10 per cent ($2.7 billion) on the 2005 announcement of McNerney's move out of 3M to the aeroplane manufacturer.

Share hikes inspired by new CEOs are now commonplace. On the 2005 announcement of Mark Hurd's joining Hewlett-Packard (HP) from NCR, HP's share price increased by 4 per cent ($4.6 billion) and NCR's decreased by 5 per cent ($0.6 billion). Research by Heidrick & Struggles in the UK covering sixteen changes in CEO within the FTSE 100 during 2005 found that the market value change on the announcement of a new CEO exceeds twice the daily fluctuation.

Getting it wrong

Of course, there's always a flip side. A fumbled CEO succession impacts not just on staff morale and business performance, but directly on a company's stock price as well. The early departure of the new CEO can also cost a company a great deal both in severance pay and dented reputation.

Yet despite their best attentions, the issue continues to bedevil companies. Richard Thoman lasted just over a year as CEO of Xerox, taking the tiller in April 1999 and relinquishing it in May 2000. During Thoman's brief watch the market capitalization of Xerox fell by around $1 billion – that's 45 per cent.

Other recent short-lived successions include M. Douglas Ivester who took charge at Coca-Cola in October 1997 and was shown the door in February 2000. Similarly, Robert Nakasone became CEO of Toys R Us in 1998, and left just 18 months later. Nakasone saw Toys R Us plunged into disarray, overtaken by Wal-Mart as the biggest toy retailer in the United States. In a reverse of the new CEO stock boost effect, Toys R Us stock jumped 50 cents on the announcement of Nakasone's departure.

Gregory Wolf lasted less than two years as CEO of Humana. Under Wolf, Humana's stock lost over half its value, a situation aggravated by a failed takeover of UnitedHealth Group (then known as United HealthCare Corp.).

Let's be clear: all of these CEOs were bright people trying their best to succeed. When things go wrong, human factors usually appear to be the nub of the problem. 'I am certain that it's the selection process that's at fault not the lack of forgiveness of the shareholders,' says Warren Bennis of the University of Southern California. 'Boards that go into rhapsodic overtures about leadership never really define what they mean by that word, nor do they pay enough attention to the human factor.'

Most bungled successions can be traced to five all-too-human failings. First, many incumbent CEOs are reluctant to give up the reins of power, either hanging on too long or trying to foist like-minded successors on to their boards. Second, boards have a tendency to appoint a safe replacement, rather than someone who will question their own role. 'Boards are rarely objective enough when recruiting CEOs,' one CEO told me. Third, boards frequently fail to define or stick to an objective set of selection criteria, allowing themselves to be swayed by force of personality. Fourth, many don't look beyond the most visible senior management candidates, and therefore fail to identify potential CEOs from the next generation of executives.

Finally, in too many cases short-term concerns are allowed to dictate the succession timetable, with the decision driven by external pressures rather than the needs of the business. Add to this the usual heady mix of executive egos, corporate politics, and greed, and you have a recipe for trouble.

When a company is performing well, succession problems tend to be a by-product of the success of the incumbent. M. Douglas Ivester, for instance, was ousted from the CEO job at Coca-Cola after a series of mis-judgements. Professor Bennis surmises that the aura of his predecessor, Roberto Goizueta, dazzled the board into doing only a cursory vetting of his nominated successor. 'Did the board really take a serious look at his capacity to work with people, to thoroughly examine his relationship with his peers and direct reports? I doubt it,' says Bennis.

Why CEOs matter

The trials and tribulations of getting the right CEO are clearly worth it. As Jim McNerney shows, CEOs can make an incredible difference to an organization. Nitin Nohria and colleagues at Harvard Business School found that the leader accounts for 14 per cent of a company's perform-ance (based on examination of a group of companies that had an average of three CEOs over twenty years; figures ranged as high as 40 per cent for the hotels sector). Other research found that nearly 50 per cent of a com-pany's reputation is linked to CEO reputation (based on a survey of 1,155 business leaders in the United States). Harvard's Rakesh Khurana esti-mates that anywhere from 30 to 40 per cent of the performance of a company is attributable to industry effects, 10 to 20 per cent to cyclical economic changes, and perhaps 10 per cent to the CEO. Ten per cent is still a great deal for one individual to be responsible for.

CEOs matter, but let's get real, they're not miracle workers. They can't change things overnight or even in weeks or months. It takes time. 'When I took the job, I thought it was a five-year project. That was a minimum expectation. It wasn't a quick fix. Three years isn't long. You can't really change a culture in that time so five years is a reasonable yardstick,' says Richard Baker, CEO of Alliance Boots.

The trouble is that time is often what CEOs have least of. The job of CEO is not blessed with a great deal of security. Indeed, it is so pressured and insecure, the remarkable thing is that people still want to be CEOs.

In these impatient times, leaders come and go – no matter whether they are leaders in politics, business, education, sport or elsewhere. Short-term pressures, already intense, are intensifying. In the business world the pressures are especially acute. Trigger-happy investors look for new blood at the slightest suggestion that the pace of growth is slackening.

The result is that the turnover of CEOs is accelerating. I read a business book recently and virtually all the business leaders quoted had moved on from their jobs. The expectation is that CEOs barely stay around long enough to change the pictures on the wall. I became CEO in September 2006. Within two weeks I was asked by analysts: 'So, how long do you want to be in the job? Your predecessors have only lasted two-and-a-half, three years.' It is a fair question, but one you'd rather not be asked. I explained that I was 41, didn't want to be out of a job when I'm 44, and I'm confident in my ability to get things done.

Even so, there are lots of statistics which make you question the wisdom of being a CEO. The average tenure of CEOs is now just 18 to 24 months. A study carried out by Murray Steele and Vivien Harrington, two academics from Cranfield School of Management, revealed that the UK's top 350 quoted companies change their CEO on average every five years. CEOs at the top 100 companies fare even worse, with 72 per cent in the role for less than five years. (Only 7 per cent of CEOs in the top 100 quoted companies have survived over ten years.)

The annual survey of CEO turnover by the consulting firm Booz Allen Hamilton makes similarly depressing reading for CEOs. Booz Allen's 2007 survey revealed that while the CEO's position remains precarious, there are signs of CEO turnover reaching a plateau. From 1995 to 2006, annual CEO turnover grew by 59 per cent. Globally, however, in 2006, 357 CEOs at the 2,500 largest public companies left office, a 1.2 per cent decrease from 2005. Turnover declined in North America, Japan and the Asia-Pacific region from the 2005 level, with a slight increase in Europe. In 2006 just over one-third of departing CEOs were forced to resign because of either poor performance or disagreements with the board. As a consolation, it is not just CEOs – the churn of chairmen and chief financial officers (CFOs) is also on the rise.

And it is not as if CEOs are especially venerated by people. They increasingly appear to be bracketed with politicians and journalists in unpopularity lists. CEOs are going through a difficult period in terms of public perception. A Bloomberg/*Los Angeles Times* poll in 2007 found that over 60 per cent of people surveyed said that CEOs are 'not too ethical' or 'not ethical at all'. Only one-third considered CEOs 'mostly ethical'. Plus, over 80 per cent believe that CEOs are paid too much.

'There is a public cynicism toward CEO leadership in the air,' says Warren Bennis. 'The corporate smell from the corporate scandals probably will affect the pool of people who want to do the job of CEO. That may not be obvious at present. But there is a stench in the air and that could affect the kinds of people who go into corporate leadership worldwide.'

All this means that there is a simmering debate about whether the job of CEO is simply too much. 'I don't think the job is impossible. CEOs just need to be more thoughtful. They need to step back and think about the nature of their business. If they do that then I think the job is doable. I actually think it's a great time to be a CEO. Sure, there are some irrational demands placed on them, but they need to think their way through that,' says management expert James Champy. 'When we read about so and so who has been brought in as CEO we read about their stock options and the company's current plight. There's very little written about their ambitions. When the CEO tries to explain his or her vision to their people in the company, it tends to be too broad – which makes it weak. It's very seldom personal to them. If you expose your personal ambitions you are much more likely to engage people than talking about vision. But CEOs are uncomfortable about that. They are fearful of making themselves vulnerable. I believe truly great managers are prepared to make themselves vulnerable. But this means they could be wrong.' The trouble is that being wrong can cost you your job.

Smelling of roses

The pressures are high but after all, most CEOs get big bucks for their trouble. Indeed, today's CEOs and senior executives are rewarded more handsomely than ever. *Forbes* magazine's 2006 survey of executive pay revealed that the average salary for the bosses of America's 500 biggest companies was $10.9 million. That's without perks, stock options, pension, change in control agreements or deferred compensation. And many CEOs who are paid millions of dollars still produce below-average returns for stockholders.

Research by the Associated Press (AP) on executive pay revealed that compensation for America's top CEOs has rocketed in the past few years. The top ten earners were from a range of industries and were all paid at least $30 million each in 2006. Of the 386 companies looked at by the AP, only six reported that their CEOs earned less than $1 million in the previous year.

High salaries are often justified by reference to the shortage of talent. This is true but not as persuasive as it might be. After all, there is a shortage of nurses in the United States at the moment – one that the Health Resources and Services Administration predicts will grow to more than 1 million nurses by 2020. The average salary for a staff nurse is about $47,000, with no stock options.

It is not finding CEOs that is hard; it is finding the *right* CEO. The reality is that CEOs are highly paid because leadership comes with a premium price tag.

One person I have talked to about this is Gerry Roche, senior chairman of Heidrick & Struggles. This bare job title does not do Gerry justice. He has more than thirty-five years of experience as a recruiter and has worked with hundreds of corporations and their boards. He has identified top executives throughout the world in almost every function and industry, probably placing more CEOs than any other recruiter. He joined Heidrick & Struggles back in 1964. Little wonder that one poll nominated Gerry as 'Recruiter of the Century'.

Gerry believes that the Renaissance men and women required as the very top CEOs are in short supply. But rarity doesn't mean they are extinct. He points to Jack Welch, Bill George of Medtronic and Jim McNerney at Boeing as proof that they do in fact exist. 'It's just they are rare breeds. These are the corporate management stars,' says Gerry. 'And, they're worth what they make in a supply and demand world. There is a lot written suggesting we overpay our chief executives. But think what we pay rock stars and football players. Think of the basketball player Lebron James who came out of high school and got a $100 million contract from Nike. Now, is that fair? Does that make sense? No. But they said, this guy's going to take the Cleveland Cavaliers to the championship, and he did. So is he worth it? It's supply and demand.'

CEOs aren't sports stars, but they are playing a high stakes game. We can talk about the rights and wrongs of CEO pay all day. But, for the people actually doing the job it is a sideshow. I have yet to meet a CEO who is motivated solely by money. Obviously money is important, but it is nowhere near as important as people might think. The challenge of leading a large organization, or turning round a failing company, or just plain competing and winning, are often more important motivating factors.

I asked Richard Baker, CEO of Alliance Boots, what motivated him. His reply was quick: 'The challenge of leadership. It is the ultimate personal test and it can be fantastically rewarding and exciting. You have enormous responsibility. Boots in the UK is a huge national institution. You are in charge of a great army. As CEO, it is your decision, but it is also a position of privilege.'

The route map

So, the appointment of a new CEO is a key moment for any organization and for the new CEO. But how does the would-be CEO get to be CEO material? What do you need to do to make the grade? The days of the CEO who worked his or her way up from the shopfloor with no college education appear to be over (if they ever existed).

The latest *Route to the Top* study by Dr Elisabeth Marx, a partner in Leadership Consulting in the London office of Heidrick & Struggles, highlights the changing career profiles of CEOs leading the UK's FTSE 100 companies. Whereas, at first sight, the profile of a typical CEO of a FTSE 100 company does not seem to have changed very much in that it is still mostly a *he*, 52 years of age and likely to come from an accountancy background; a closer analysis of the data shows a remarkable shift in the career pattern and appointment of CEOs.

> The **international experience** of CEOs has increased quite dramatically over the years. Whereas, in 1996, only 42 per cent of CEOs of FTSE 100 companies had international experience (defined as having had an overseas assignment), this figure rose to 61 per cent in 2002 and to 79 per cent in 2005. This clearly underpins the requirement of an international background for the top positions in this country. The majority of the international experience was gained in North America and Europe, less so in the growth regions of Asia and South America.

> **Internal promotion**. The ratio of internal promotion versus external recruitment has changed over the years. Whereas in 1996 72 per cent of CEOs were internally promoted, this figure rose to 77 per cent in 2002, suggesting more systematic succession planning and maybe also a more risk-averse appointment process. The percentage of internally promoted CEOs had fallen to 69 per cent by 2005, indicating a trend for more external CEO searches.

> **Nationality**. Seventy-two per cent of CEOs are British, the other 28 per cent of FTSE 100 CEOs come from outside the UK. The majority of these are from the United States followed by Europe, Australia and South Africa.

> **Functional background**. A finance/accounting background is still the most frequent route to the top in the UK. For example, in 1996, 24 per cent of CEOs had a finance/accounting background. This increased to a startling 41 per cent by 2002, raising the question of whether UK boardrooms are diverse enough in terms of functional background. In 2005, 38 per cent of CEOs had a finance/accounting background, followed by sales/marketing (23 per cent) and general management (18 per cent).

> **Education**. In 1996, over one-third (37 per cent) of FTSE 100 CEOs did not have a university degree. This pattern has changed dramatically: in 2002 only 11 per cent of CEOs had no university degree, and in 2005 this figure was at 12 per cent. The majority of CEOs have university degrees and are therefore closer now to their European counterparts in terms of academic qualifications.

> **Oxbridge background**. Another interesting shift is in the prevalence of Oxbridge backgrounds. In 1996, 19 per cent of CEOs had an Oxbridge education. Some might expect an elitist background to decrease but this is not the case. In 2005, 22 per cent of FTSE 100 CEOs had an Oxbridge background (three of whom have additional Harvard degrees). If we include a Harvard education, given the high number of foreign CEOs, the combined Oxbridge/Harvard background climbs to 28 per cent.

> **Age**. As in 2002, the average age of a CEO is still 52, slightly lower than the 55 average in 1996. The 1996 analysis identified a 'super group' of young CEOs up to age 45. The number of young super-CEOs was 6 in 1996, 13 in 2002 and is now 10.

Professor Monika Hamori at the Instituto de Empresa Business School in Madrid has carried out research on career paths. In a major study she analysed the CVs of the CEOs of the 500 largest companies in both the United States and Europe (1,000 in all).

Professor Hamori's study suggests that career paths have changed in the past decade in four important ways. First, the loyal company man or woman is increasingly rare. The second career shift is that executives are evaluated against much higher, more rigorous performance standards. Booz Allen Hamilton's annual CEO study shows that the percentage of CEOs dismissed for performance-based reasons has quadrupled since the mid-1990s.

The third change is a move towards younger appointments based on merit. 'Today's corporate landscape presents greater opportunities for those who want to reach the top of corporate hierarchies,' says Professor Hamori. 'My research with Professor Peter Cappelli at Wharton [School, University of Pennsylvania] shows that high performers are appointed to CEO and executive positions about four years younger than they were 20 years ago.'

The final change, she says, is that single-industry and single-job-function careers are in decline. 'Executives who have worked in multiple industries and multiple job functions – and therefore have an eclectic management experience – are much more appreciated and in demand today than a couple of years ago,' she says. 'Single-function executives represent a tiny minority these days and their proportion keeps on decreasing.'

My route

In truth there is no uncomplicated answer to how you should go about building a career which leads to the CEO job. There are hundreds of books about careers. And yet no one I ever meet has a career like the ones you read about. In the books, careers are planned, orderly, linear. One thing leads to another. If you can pull it off, it's quite an achievement, but in my experience careers are messy, spontaneous and exciting. Careers are actually the story of your life.

I am CEO of the world's top executive search firm (but then, I'm biased). My route to this job doesn't read like a book. Though my starting point was a book. I was working in banking in the United States and reading a book which argued that learning Japanese would be crucial to businesses of the future. At the time this made sense. Japan was the industrial jugger-naut of the day. Then I got a call from my old college room-mate who happened to be living in Japan. He told me about a teaching job over there and asked me to come over. That was November.

By 7 January I was out in the middle of the Japanese countryside. Nobody spoke English. Japanese restaurateurs put models of food in their windows and so, to order a meal, I had to take the restaurant owners outside and point at what I wanted. Every day I ended up eating noodles – an immediate lesson in the importance of communication and the limitations of noodles as a diet. After ten days I was tired of noodles and ready to go home.

In time, I made progress, taught at a kindergarten and continued to study Japanese. In 1992 I moved to Tokyo and realized I wanted to get some working experience in Japan before I went back to the United States. I approached a headhunting company to try to get a job in banking. They offered me a job with them. I wasn't keen, but I had very little money so took the job. My thinking was that I'd work a few months, save some money and then look elsewhere. But, after three months I was really enjoying the job and the opportunity it gave me to engage with people and help organizations.

Later, I returned to New York for a couple of years and was then hired by PA Consulting to run its Tokyo operation. From there I joined Heidrick & Struggles, to set up its Financial Services Practice in Japan. At 32 years old I was very young for such a job and there was some push-back from a number of senior people because they didn't feel I was experienced enough. (One advantage I have always had is looking older than I actually am.)

While working at Heidrick & Struggles I did an MBA at Duke University's Fuqua Business School. I got up at 5.30 each morning to study for a couple of hours before work and then studied 8–10 hours on the weekend. Thank goodness I only had one child at that time. In September 2002 I became head of Asia-Pacific for the firm and in 2005 I combined this role with leading the firm in Europe, the Middle East and Africa.

Truth be told, I never dreamt of becoming CEO. Before I was asked to run Asia-Pacific for Heidrick & Struggles, leadership was just not some-thing I was interested in. I remember saying to the person who was running Asia at the time I was asked to take over, 'You could have told me Martians had landed outside and I would have been less surprised than you asking me to take on this role.' I was surprised because I simply hadn't thought of it.

When the CEO job came up with the entire company I was approached as an internal candidate. As is usually the case, there were also some external candidates. For any CEO candidate, even becoming part of the process is a big decision. When you're asked to compete you have to think what's right for the business at the time, what's right for yourself and what's right for your family. I needed to think: if they hire someone else, do I leave the firm, because I've been here nine years? For the first time I was thinking about leaving the firm that I love. This is a major struggle as an individual because you see the changes you've already made and you know what you would do if you got the CEO role. But are you ready to really put yourself on the line? In the final analysis, the only person who can answer this is you.

In my case, I realized I was still young and could perhaps get a CEO job later on. I could have waited a couple of years. From a personal view, my family loved England, I loved living there, so it was personally a big decision (because I knew it would mean a relocation to the company HQ in Chicago). I also had a couple of other organizations talking to me about doing something else – and I think most CEOs have this just before they are signed up.

I went through the same interviewing process as everyone else. I met every member of the board individually – though I was helped by having attended a few board meetings previously so I knew each one of them.

It was actually a very useful process because it allowed me to be introspective. The board members grilled me about my weaknesses (and told me what they believed my weaknesses were), and asked me how I was going to address them. When you think that very few senior executives get formal career coaching and assessment, at that stage in my career it was very beneficial. It made me think about myself, the firm and what it was I needed to do to grow as a leader and as a person. I still have those thoughts and intentions written down.

Career logistics

So, that's how I became a CEO. I'm not saying that's the way you should do it. And I don't want to sound glib. The point is that I didn't really think and believe I would be CEO until the phone call came through confirming it.

And I remember that phone call well. I was sitting in my office in London when the phone rang. I picked it up and there was a female voice saying, 'Could you hold for Dick Beattie, please' (chairman of Simpson Thacher & Bartlett LPP and lead director of Heidrick & Struggles) – I knew what this was about! The ten seconds it took to connect us were the longest of my life: time seemed to come to a total halt. And then there was Dick, saying, 'Kevin, we would like to offer you the job of CEO.' It was only then I believed I could ever be a CEO. I saw Dick in an elevator a few weeks after the call and he laughed as he remembered that conversation. 'I really got you that day, didn't I?' Yes, Dick, you certainly did.

Among the most fascinating of the CEOs I talked to during the research for this book was Carlos Ghosn, president and CEO of auto manufacturer Nissan and president and CEO of Renault. Carlos is the benchmark for the truly global, successful CEO. He is Brazilian-born but was brought up in Lebanon and educated in France. His career has been equally mobile. He worked with Michelin for eighteen years. First he was a plant manager in Le Puy, France; then head of research and development for industrial tyres in Ladoux, France; and then he was chief operating officer of Michelin's South American activities based in Brazil. From there he became chairman and CEO of Michelin North America. There he restructured the company after it acquired the Uniroyal Goodrich Tire Company in 1990.

He went on in 1996 to become executive vice president of the Renault Group. As well as supervising Renault activities in the Mercosur, he was responsible for advanced research, car engineering and development, car manufacturing, power train operations and purchasing. He joined Nissan as its chief operating officer in June 1999, became its president in June 2000 and was named CEO in June 2001. At the time he joined, Nissan was $20 billion in debt and only three of its 48 models were generating a profit. Ghosn claimed that Nissan would have no net debt by 2005. One year after he arrived, Nissan's net profit climbed to $2.7 billion from a loss of $6.1 billion in the previous year. He also became president of Renault in May 2005.

Carlos Ghosn's route to the top is a classic experience-based one. Over the past thirty years he has worked and led throughout the world in a variety of roles and functions. It is a pattern you see time and time again among CEOs. It doesn't matter which sector they come from, most have clocked up a lot of experience in lots of different businesses and business functions.

Take Gary Knell. He is CEO of Sesame Workshop, the not-for-profit educational organization behind Sesame Street. His business is about a million miles distant from Carlos Ghosn's world in the automotive industry but, talking to Gary, it is clear that the issues are often similar, and how you get to the top remarkably similar. 'In a non-profit there is what I would call a double bottom line: a quantitative set of measures which are probably consistent with the for profit world and then an expectation that you're making an impact on society. If you're not making that impact, you're not going to get the income you need to survive,' Gary explains.

I then asked him about how he came to arrive at Sesame Workshop. 'In some ways there was a natural progression in my career. I have a background originally in journalism and law and politics. So, I was working in Washington as a staff counsel on the US Senate Judiciary Committee back in the late 1970s and proceeded on to work in public broadcasting where I got to really know the television business at WNET/Channel 13 in New York. Then I jumped over to Sesame Workshop, in the business affairs and legal unit, and was then promoted to chief administrative officer. This helped me cover a lot of the backbone of the organization and learn everything, from information systems to marketing to human resources and everything else and being part of the senior executive team. It gave me the experience to know what makes the corporation run and the importance of managing people. That led to a progression and some global experience and then finally becoming CEO.'

Career evolution

Another CEO I talked to about career progression was Monika Ribar, president and CEO of Panalpina, the global transport and logistics company which employs 14,000 people and operates a network of about 500 offices with branches in 90 countries. Monika took over as CEO in 2006 at the age of 47 after being the company's CIO (chief information officer) and then CFO. Monika's career has built up to becoming CEO. Her accumulated experiences helped make her a natural CEO candidate. But this was, she points out, more of a process of evolution than a plan.

'Over the last five or six years, I have said that if I got the opportunity I would like to manage a company and to have the full responsibility of being CEO. It was not something I was totally fixed on. But I think I have learnt a lot, I have seen a lot, and I think I could do the job in a slightly different way,' she says.

But, even after sixteen years with the company and a huge variety of experience Monika believes that the CEO job is unique. 'I think that the CFO job in a company is very, very important job, but still you are sharing responsibility. As the CEO it's you. Period.'

This certainly struck a chord with my own experience. As you grow up in a firm, you encounter a lot of different individuals, but they tend only to look at their piece of the puzzle, whether it's finance, operations or technology. As CEO you find you have to look at the whole organization. And you quickly realize that if you pull one lever it affects everything else.

Monika Ribar believes that her background in financial control encouraged her to look at the company in broader terms, and her range of experience within the company was also helpful. 'I did different jobs. I did a lot of projects, including IT which is very important for a logistics company. And now, being the CEO, one of the main things is to put the right people in the right positions because you can't do it yourself any more. Take IT, I don't have a technical background at all and there were people who were probably not that happy when I took over as CIO, but I managed and nobody left. The people who were not happy are still here and they were very unhappy when I left IT. So I think I have learnt to deal with people and to motivate them whatever their likes and dislikes.'

Get on with the job

Talking to people it is evident that the CEO job suddenly becomes clear and achievable, like a summit above the clouds. The CEOs I have met are ambitious, but they have not made their ambition the cornerstone of their being and their work.

Take Richard Baker, CEO of Alliance Boots. After Richard took over as CEO he led Boots to a successful merger with Alliance UniChem. 'I was never hung up on the title of CEO,' he told me. 'From an early age I organized things – whether it was at the cub scouts or on the sports field. I was organizing, communicating and leading. It was a logical conclusion to become a CEO. I enjoy leading.'

Driven and ambitious, some are natural leaders, but all would-be CEOs ensure that they deliver on the job in hand. Gerry Roche sums this up in characteristically robust fashion: 'The best way to get your next job is to do a good job at the job you're in, and not be distracted by positioning and posturing yourself for the next role. The minute you start distracting yourself from your current responsibilities to choreograph your next job the trouble can start. What we see all the time is people who come to us and say I have a good job where I am as a COO [chief operating officer] but I want to be a CEO, can you help me do that? And they do that with us and with all our competitors. We wind up thinking that he's spending more time on where he's going than succeeding where he is.

My thinking is that the best way to get a promotion or get a new job is to excel at what you're doing. Trust me, we will find you. Your managers will wind up saying, "Hey, there's a guy down there who's knocking the ball out of the park like crazy, let's put him into finance for a while and round him out, so that when we're looking for our next president, he's a candidate."

That's the way it usually happens and it should happen. You can't allow your-self to get distracted with politicking, choreographing and stylizing for the future at the expense of short-changing the job for which you are responsi-ble. At the same time, you need to do some strategic planning of your own and say, "Hey, if I'm ever going to get to run GE, I'd better go get a tour in finance and in strategic planning, running a profit centre alone won't do it."

In terms of managing my own career, I measured it by my performance. I did what was asked of me to the very best of my abilities, for my bosses and for my clients. I just got on with the job at hand and wasn't looking at the horizon all the time.

In the ascendancy

As Gerry Roche suggests, the normal journey to top management is to rise up through operations, not necessarily through staff positions. Future CEOs generally have experience running profit centres. Think of Carlos Ghosn's career progression. At GE all those in the frame to succeed Jack Welch – Jeff Imelt, Jim McNerney, Bob Nardelli (who just became CEO of Chrysler) and so on – had all run large profit centres.

Some rise via the job of COO. 'The single most dominant functional background for a chief operating officer is running things, execution. When you're picking a COO the questions are: does this person know the elements of getting a job done, can he execute that job, can he do things, can he see that things are done, can he produce the bottom line? Those are the talents of a COO,' says Gerry Roche.

Running different profit centres is a good idea but, equally, remember there is no cookie-cutter template for the CEO. Steve Tappin leads Heidrick & Struggles' CEO and board practice in the UK. To keep up to date with the marketplace, during 2007 he interviewed the CEOs of 67 of the FTSE 100. Steve's conclusions are many, intriguing and varied. 'I think what was sur-prising was just the diversity of the different types of CEOs,' he told me. 'I think you can look at CEOs by situation. There are some CEOs who are very entrepreneurial – in the UK there is Charlie Dunstone at Carphone Warehouse and WPP's Martin Sorrell. There are other CEOs, like Allan Leighton, who are very good in turnarounds, and in terms of operational performance improvement. Then there's another group who are interna-tional consolidators – people like John Browne during his time at BP – and there are business transformers who come in, refocus the business, and transform it. Some CEOs are better in certain types of situations.'

In his research, Steve Tappin differentiates between the CEOs who could be termed 'professional managers' and those who are first and foremost leaders. He explains: 'Professional managers could be seen as a negative term, but what I mean by that is that they're generalists. They're pretty good at strategy, pretty good with people, pretty good at execution, and they build a good team around them, and they succeed in that way. And I think there's also a group of CEOs that are very strong leaders. Some of the best CEOs have the appetite to lead from the front when they need to, and make some of the important calls for the business, but also, are equally comfortable in developing other leaders, empowering them, training them in the culture for them to actually lead, to lead within a business. And, I think, there's a small group of people who can do that. I think for a lot of them the root of their success lies in some of their personal qualities. Increasingly, they aren't just having a big idea, it's more around how you can keep driving an organization forward.'

Similarly, Gerry Roche's starting point for all his work is that every single executive is different. 'I have a line that I like a lot. Oliver Wendell Holmes said "No generality is worth a damn, including this one." Well, I know a lot of CEOs and no two of them are alike.'

The message is clear: *vive la difference*! In their book *Why Should Anyone Be Led By You?*, Rob Goffee and Gareth Jones have distilled this down to the simple advice: 'Be yourself – more – with skill.'

The glass ceiling remains

One thing I would like to mention at this stage is the continuing absence of women from the top job in the business world. The Lehman Brothers Centre for Women in Business surveyed 61 European companies and other organizations to determine how they measure and manage gender issues. Amazingly, only 15 per cent of senior executive positions in Europe are held by women. (The encouraging news in Europe is that 50–60 per cent of graduate recruits joining European businesses are now women, though it is still anticipated that women will occupy only 20 per cent of senior roles by 2017.)

The reasons for the continuing paucity of women at the top of organizations are explained by Lynda Gratton, professor of management practice at London Business School. 'There is a clear gap between policy rhetoric and practical reality. Policies such as flexible working and part-time working can be crucial to women as they move up the corporate ladder. Yet while most companies have these policies, few actually use them. Less than 10 per cent of female managers actually adopt flexible working, and less than 20 per cent of managers and senior executives work part time.

'The challenge here is not creating the policy, but rather establishing an environment in which it is seen to be legitimate to take these options. Creating a place where both men and women feel able to work flexibly would do much to reduce the leaky pipeline of female talent, and indeed create more humane places of work for men.' Professor Gratton also laments the lack of women at the world's business schools – typically 20 per cent, she estimates.

Little wonder that the women at the top of organizations are usually remarkable and that their experiences are very different from those of their male colleagues. Monika Ribar of Panalpina admits that being a lone woman in a room full of men is hardly a new experience for her. At her business school, women made up a mere 14 per cent of students. 'You need to know people and this is probably easier for a man to get into than for a woman. If a colleague CEO asks me for lunch or for dinner, it's a different story if you do that as a man and a woman or if you do that as two men or two women. Something which is in the man's community totally normal, all of a sudden gets viewed differently. Our society has to get used to this and be able to deal with it as normal.'

Learning . . . always

The key thing in developing as a potential and actual CEO is a willingness to learn as you go along. I learnt a great deal in my first Asia-Pacific leadership role – about restructuring, letting people go, rebuilding, entering new markets and handling personalities. That is when I began to learn about change and how people handle it. If you want to change the firm and the organization, sometimes it means taking people out, and that never gets any easier. I also learnt the importance of providing coaching and feedback to individuals. You need to be direct from the beginning. I used to try to work with people and say, 'Look, could you think about doing this', or 'Would you mind doing that' – and they wouldn't get the message. I learnt that, as uncomfortable as it is, you must be direct and clear. As a leader there are more and more demands on your time, and if you have to keep going back and having the same conversations over and over again, you will simply run out of time. Being direct isn't easy. I used to find it uncomfortable, particularly when giving people bad news, but you learn that it is the way to handle your time, to handle change and to get things done.

Key points

> CEO tenure is shortening. This is a reality and any would-be CEO has to bear it in mind. Before applying or agreeing to become a CEO, they must think of what the job entails, the pressures that come with it, and whether at this stage in their career they are ready for it.

> There is no one-size-fits-all instant career guide if you want to become a CEO. Every career and CEO is different.

> But it is worth remembering that most successful CEOs learn as they go along. They work hard at learning always. They are also skilled at execution but, critically, combine this with knowledge of planning and strategy.

Resources

Bennis, Warren and O'Toole, James, 'Don't hire the wrong CEO', *Harvard Business Review,* May 2000.

Bloomberg News, 'Americans in poll hit ethics, pay of CEOs', *Boston Globe*, 14 June 2007.

Burson Marsteller, *Building CEO Capital,* 2001.

Champy, James and Nohria, Nitin, *The Arc of Ambition,* Perseus, 2001.

Forbes magazine executive pay report 2006. Available at www.forbes.com/2006/04/17/06ceo_ceo-compensation_land.html

George, Bill, Gergen, David, and Sims, David, *True North: Discover Your Authentic Leadership,* Jossey-Bass, 2007.

Ghosn, Carlos and Ries, Philippe, *Shift: Inside Nissan's Historic Revival*, Currency, 2006.

Goffee, Rob and Jones, Gareth, *Why Should Anyone Be Led By You?*, Harvard Business School Press, 2006.

Gratton, Lynda, *Hot Spots*, Berrett Koehler, 2007.

Hamori, Monika and Capelli, Peter, 'The path to the top', NBER Working Paper, May 2004.

Khurana, Rhakesh, 'The curse of the superstar CEO', *Harvard Business Review*, September 2002.

Knowledge@Wharton, 'Want to win? Here's some practical advice from Jack Welch', 1 June 2005.

Lucier, Chuck, Wheeler, Steven and Habbel, Rolf, 'CEO Succession 2006: the era of the inclusive leader', Booz Allen's annual CEO succession study', *Strategy+Business*, Summer 2007.

Marx, Elisabeth, *Route to the Top*, Heidrick & Struggles, 2006.

Steele, Murray, 'Challenges of leadership: the life and times of the CEO', Cranfield School of Management Centre for Business Performance WWW.

The Economist, 'Tough at the top', 23 October 2003.

Useem, Jerry, 'Jim McNerney thinks he can turn 3M from a good company into a great one – with a little help from his former employer, General Electric', *Fortune*, 8 December 2002.

Chapter 2

My first 100 days

There are many books about what CEOs should and should not do when they take over. One hundred days is only a short time, and far shorter when everyone inside the company and out is watching your every move. So, what does the new CEO need to do before taking the job and when the first day beckons?

I used almost all of the first 100 days to talk to people in operations. I went to the company's battlefields rather than staying at head office and getting reports from a lot of managers. I went to the battlefields and talked to the managers and the soldiers.

Takeshi Niinami, CEO, Lawson

Tone setting

Seung-Yu Kim became CEO of the Hana Financial Group in Korea in 1997. The timing was not auspicious. 'Our economy was really in trouble. Our currency was overvalued and in my first 100 days twelve of the thirty biggest Korean conglomerates were bankrupted. The last one was Kia Motors which we had a big exposure to. It went bankrupt on 20 July. I still remember the date.'

Seung-Yu Kim had been with Hana since the time it had a mere twenty people. Hana developed its commercial banking in the early 1990s and Seung-Yu Kim was well placed because he had prior experience and a network in commercial banking. This did not, however, prepare him for taking over a company at the height of a far-reaching economic crisis. Faced with a crisis, Seung-Yu Kim focused on 'awakening my people', reshaping and restructuring.

From the start he worked at making all employees feel appreciated. After taking over as CEO in February, he led the purchase of a training centre in April. 'At the time we had less than 1,000 people so every week, in the evening, I met with some of them. In my first 100 days in particular I tried to appreciate them one by one.'

Surrounded by crisis, Seung-Yu Kim increased salaries by a mere 2 per cent in 1997, put his own pay rise on hold and cut costs. 'For example, I took economy class when I had a business trip overseas. Most CEOs travel first class, but this was part of me showing my people how much I appreciated and valued them. My people followed me and trusted me, and that's why we overcame the financial crisis.' When Seung-Yu Kim insisted on flying economy, the airlines, aware of why he was flying economy, used to leave the neighbouring seat vacant.

Seung-Yu Kim was in the habit of heading home at nine or ten o'clock at night. On his way home, if he saw any of the bank's branches with their lights on he stopped off and paid a visit. People working extra hours were regularly treated to pizzas courtesy of the CEO. The pizzas came with a message. 'Whenever I made a surprise visit to our branches, I highlighted the significance of our customers. I always tried to tell people that our shareholders could leave us at any time were we not profitable, but our customers would stay with us if we did our best for them. I also reminded them that they didn't need to look for market trends as market demand is nothing but the products and services which customers want us to provide them. They listened to me. And, now, the strong customer/market-oriented philosophy of the early days of Hana Bank has become the core value of the entire Group.'

What are you walking into?

It is never easy starting a new job. There are new people, a new office, new expectations. For the CEO these issues are magnified. People are watching and waiting. It is like being in a goldfish bowl – perhaps that's why so many executive offices have fish tanks.

The reality can be daunting. The money may be good but job security is low and diminishing, and the job itself rarely presents a clean and happy start. Takeshi Niinami, CEO of convenience store chain Lawson (30 per cent owned by Mitsubishi), recalls his early days as CEO with mixed emotions. 'I think during the first 100 days I was a very severe leader. I made cuts and, from the employees' point of view, I was a bad leader. I'd come from a big company, Mitsubishi, and nobody knew who I was. The first 100 days were really a mistake in terms of morale and motivating people. I couldn't motivate people at all.'

Takeshi's honesty is brutal, but the situation he inherited was bad and worsening. 'The company was not doing very well. When I arrived profits were on their way to sinking from $405 million to $340 million. But there was no feeling of crisis among people. They thought, we're still making profits, what's wrong? It was very hard to create a feeling that there was a crisis among the rank and file. It was very difficult.'

The challenging truth experienced by countless new CEOs is that if a company needs a CEO, there is often – not always – a problem. Of course, you know that problems exist. Every company in the world has problems. They wouldn't have recruited a new CEO if everything was fine. But, rest assured, the problems are always worse than you think. So, new leaders regularly walk into unpredictable and unstable situations. Morale may be low. Employees – and shareholders – are confused about the organization's direction. Performance is likely to be down. Enter a new leader – often into a new organization – frequently into a new industry.

And then there's the final pressure point: everyone expects the CEO to put his or her mark on the organization within 100 days.

The first 100 days of a leader's tenure is much commented on. Indeed, the time the CEO has to make an impact is decreasing. 'Boards are more willing to toss people out and are giving CEOs a much shorter leash. Many senior executives feel they have a much shorter time frame to prove themselves,' says former Harvard Business School and INSEAD professor Michael Watkins, author of *The First 90 Days*. (Note the book title: that's another ten days gone.)

But while there is less time to make an impression, there is no mythical day when things have to be done by. Leadership is no longer neatly linear

– if it ever was. A CEO's first period in charge is a roller coaster. Before boarding a roller coaster it is advisable to have an idea of what you are letting yourself in for. By understanding the process, CEOs are likely to cope with its ups and downs far more effectively.

My first 100

Hands up. I admit that I have all these books sitting on my bookcase telling what the first 90 or 100 days should consist of. You know it's going to be bad – you know there will need to be restructuring of the business, pieces of the business that need turning around, functions that need changing and improving, and people decisions to make – but until you actually sit down on the first day and see it first hand, until you lift up the covers, you're not going to really understand the challenge.

My own plan for the first 100 days as CEO was to figure out who the right people were and to establish whether I had enough of the right people to get us where we needed to go. I had a very clear idea about the direction of the firm, and where I wanted to go. The unknown piece at the beginning, even as an insider, is the people. I think most CEOs would agree that in these early days you find 20 per cent of individuals want to embrace change and get there, 60 per cent can go either way, and 20 per cent probably have to go because they don't want to change and will do anything they can to throw roadblocks up.

At the same time as looking internally, I was very keen to remain outward facing. I wanted to keep up my client work as I felt we were too inward facing as a firm. But even though you endeavour to go and do that, you realize the internal part of the job needs lots more attention. It is like the game whack-a-mole: every time you sort one thing out something else pops up, and I don't think that ever stops. Events dictate the pace. Always.

There is a great story about the British prime minister Harold Macmillan. He was asked what made the job of prime minister difficult. 'Events, dear boy, events,' he replied. Every CEO knows the feeling.

I remember my first week, I had a great opening 24, even 36, hours with people calling and congratulating and expressing how hopeful they were. I had the people in Asia whom I had grown up with, and the people in EMEA I had been working with, all calling me. Being an American out of America, the Americans were a little more unsure. Although I sound American – I am an American – after twelve years away, my fellow countrymen tend not to be sure I'm one of them any longer. Many people view me as stateless rather than an American. So, from the first you have to be aware of how you're perceived and thought of. How can you reassure people? Should you reassure them or is it better that you're slightly distant?

Like most CEOs, I put more pressure on myself than anyone else does – and particularly in those first 100 days you know people are giving you their time and trust but they want action and you need to deliver. Every time a new leader comes in there is hope that they will change things for the better, but the leader needs to understand that the individual doesn't particularly want the change to affect them personally. People want change, people want action but they don't like to deal with it directly.

Looking back now, after nine months (and counting), I don't think I'd do anything differently in terms of those first 100 days. Maybe I would have put less pressure on myself in those first months – because actually the pressure never lets up, and you just need to keep figuring out what's going on, put your head down and get things done.

The art of preparation

The more I talked to other CEOs, the more it became clear that how you start is critical. Take Richard Baker who was 40 when he took over as CEO of Boots, which later became Alliance Boots. Richard had worked at Mars, where he was sales director, and Asda beforehand. He was highly experienced and had been COO at Asda. Even so, he admits that he was 'not at all prepared' for the rigours of being a CEO. 'Even as a COO you tend to stick to a few disciplines. You're at the heart of the action, but you don't need to know how a financial audit works, for example. I'd worked on brands, products and operations, but knew little of IT, finance, HR and so on. It was a big leap and that's why it is the ultimate test. You come up through organizations and develop a particular competence and then you find yourself running the show. That's the same for most CEOs.'

In a business like Alliance Boots, Richard has to deal with a whole range of technical support functions which are fundamental to the business. As CEO he soon found himself signing off huge investments in IT with limited knowledge of the technical detail.

Given that as a new CEO you are suddenly thrust into such alien territory, how do you cope? 'You need good general management skills and judgement,' says Richard Baker. 'And people you can trust, with the technical competence required by the business. The big word is trust. You've got to get a team of people together you can trust.'

Before taking over at Alliance Boots, Richard had a four-month break to contemplate the job ahead. This is not an unusual situation. I was interested as to how he spent this time. It must, I thought, be a curious period. The CEO in waiting is in limbo, watching and hoping, with limited opportunities to learn more or get involved. Richard spent his time talking to people whose judgement he trusted. He talked to suppliers to the company whom he already knew and visited the company's shops to have a look round. He talked to other CEOs and took as much advice as possible. He learnt about the business from the outside in.

The result of all this was that when he started his new job, Richard Baker had a plan for the first two or three weeks. 'In the first two weeks I interviewed all of the top thirty people at the company,' he recalls. 'I had a formal questionnaire so they were all asked the same questions. I wanted to find out what they thought worked well and what they would do in my position. They were simple, open questions, and from that I got a good consensus as to what we needed to do. Perhaps twenty-five out of the thirty were saying much the same thing.'

Richard was able to largely keep to his plan in the first few weeks. No sudden crises materialized. He then organized a detailed review of the company's top management team by a recruitment expert. Managers were in effect interviewed for their own jobs. Based on this work and Richard's judgements, changes were made to the management team within the first six weeks.

'The first 100 days really are critical. You set the tone,' says Richard. 'At the first meetings you can almost see people's antennae twitching. People are looking to see whether you're relaxed, impatient and so on. First impressions are critical. If you think about it, you do most things once in 100 days.'

Flashpoints may emerge in the unlikeliest of places – at Boots, Richard Baker arrived wearing a collar and tie as he had always done in his previous companies, but the dress culture at Boots was more informal. He was asked for his opinion on the dress code. His four months of preparation hadn't covered this issue. 'I hadn't planned it but said I thought people weren't dressed professionally enough. We were in a war and I expected people to be dressed for battle. Eventually I had to sit some of the people down and tell them that was a rule. It was a diktat. That sort of thing sets the tone.'

The same but different

'No one trains you to be a CEO,' Gary Knell, CEO of Sesame Workshop told me. 'I think the first day you look to your left, you look to your right and all of a sudden everyone's looking at you. It is somewhat lonely, at least certainly in the beginning. All of a sudden you've got to make some judgements and trust that you are getting advice from the variety of quarters that you need. The key is having people whom you trust around you who are going to tell you objectively what's happening.

'I think the importance of a listening tour shouldn't be underestimated. Even though I was an insider, in that I knew the place and the culture, when you're sitting at the top, people aren't going to open to you in the way that they want to open up to you as a peer. I think it's important that you are spending some time to really learn, from that top position, what are the critical issues and where are the risks and opportunities. After three months or so you can really apply some change and make some decisions. The other thing that certainly happened in my case, and probably tends to happen more than is written about, is things are thrown at you in those first 100 days. For 100 days or 90 days or 60 days you've got to actually get right into the thick of the stuff and start making some decisions.

'People test you. They want to test what you're made of in the sense that, is this going to be somebody who is going to make decisions quickly or take a lot of time or procrastinate? They want to test your style. People who were formerly your peers are going to look at you in a much different way. Maybe some of them were rivals for the job and have some sort of hurt feelings about it. So, it's finding a way to raise people's vision and trying to bring some closure on the process of selection and say, okay, that's been done, we've got to focus now on the future of the company, and you want to inspire people to be part of that solution.'

Among the CEOs I talked to about the first 100 days was Monika Ribar. Monika's situation was somewhat unusual in that it was announced that she was to become CEO of Panalpina in June 2006 and she actually began the job in October. This poses a slightly different challenge in that she had a pre-100 days before the first 100 days actually began.

'Whatever I did after June was to some extent looked at as if I was doing it as the CEO. It changes from the day you are announced. People react differently, they look at you differently. I don't think that I have changed, but it's the job. When it came to 1 October, I don't think that I did anything differently. Of course, I didn't take care of the CFO stuff, because I had found my CFO. For me it was very important that I started to think about how to organize myself. People were always asking me, will you work more now? And I said, no, I can't work more, but I have to work differently. This is certainly something which I gave a lot of thought to. How do I organize myself? What is my agenda?'

Having clarified her modus operandi and her expectations, Monika brought together her management team three months into her time as CEO. 'It took one strategy meeting, which was very hard for me because I needed to align them on the same targets. And when they realized that I'm not against them, that I can help them and that I'm not coming in and changing everything, that I'm interested and that I want to learn and that I don't come and say, you know what, I know it better than you do. I think this convinced them she wants to help us; she has a clear target; she's communicating very clearly. Let's give it a try.'

Understand the process

For a CEO to emerge unscathed at the end of their first 100 days takes focus, energy and luck. I found that it takes a while to move from defence to offence.

As Monika Ribar makes clear, there are always tough decisions to be made. The starting point, however, if CEOs are to survive and, eventually, thrive is first to understand the process which they will experience. Most of the many books about leadership focus on personality characteristics. Clearly, these are important but it is also vital that leaders have some understanding of the process of leadership – the timescales that will affect them and the likely highs and lows. These are particularly acute over the first few days, weeks and months in a new leadership role.

The process has four phases: anticipation, exploration, building and contributing.

Anticipation

Even before starting work, it is important that any leader develops an entry strategy, as Richard Baker showed us so clearly. They must look at their role, set expectations, discuss any issues which need immediate clarity, and enter into an honest exchange of views and hopes. Clearly, they have to be careful not to overplay their hand or to become too involved too soon. But, the tone can be set even before entering the building.

Exploration

The timelines are fairly consistent. During the first 90 days of a new leader's tenure there is a honeymoon period – though honeymoons, like job tenure, are shortening dramatically. Throughout this time, leaders get to know the organization, the people and the management team. This is the exploration phase. At this point the board offers long-term support and promises whatever resources are required.

Even so, as I experienced, the first period is one of intense pressure. There may be support from elsewhere, but leaders tend, initially at least, to put pressure on themselves. They have a new job and a new challenge and they feel it is down to them to deliver. If you really, really want to be a CEO, that personal pressure can actually be incredibly intense. After all, you may have spent the best part of thirty years acquiring the skills and experience to become a CEO. You have a lot of sweat invested in the job. You desperately want to make it work. And – CEOs are only human – you are fearful of failure. You can't bear the thought of screwing it up. All that time and energy, all those dreams, disappearing into well-publicized smoke.

They are right to feel pressured. Research suggests that the roots of failure can be traced to what happens within the first fifteen days. Common causes of this are trying to do too much too soon; failing to assimilate the culture; failing to adapt leadership and management styles; and insufficient analysis and planning. And I come from a generation which didn't grow up with multitasking! We used to joke about not being able to walk down the street and chew gum at the same time. Now you've got your BlackBerry, tickers on the computer screen, earphones in, phone ringing. I grew up in a generation of black-and-white TVs; now everything is in high definition touchscreen technicolour. This only serves to crank up the pressure.

None of this makes life easy for the new CEO. The challenge is that while leaders are often hired to achieve change, there is always resistance when change actually happens. Leaders can find themselves firmly wedged between the proverbial rock and a hard place. Failure is clearly bad for the individual and expensive for the company – it has been estimated that the cost of a failed hire is at least four times salary and bonus.

Building

And then the pressure balance changes. The building stage – three to fourteen months – marks a shift in emphasis. The leader has assembled a team and the onus is on the team to deliver. This is a time when the leader can encounter emotional lows. After the initial rush of excitement, it is easy to feel physically and mentally exhausted. Difficult decisions still need to be made. The leader may need to act on people who are clearly in the wrong roles or simply not up to the tasks required.

'There are a lot of CEOs who start off and get some initial momentum. They launch a lot of initiatives, and make some changes, like disposing of things, or changing the people at the top. And they get into that in the first six months. But, I think there's a period after that where they either get a grip of the company and start to lead it, or they're just constantly firefighting and eventually fail in the role,' says Steve Tappin. 'I think there's a six- to nine-months window, a window with investors, and within the company, where you can make some initial changes that are relatively straightforward. But, I think the challenge is the next period.'

Contributing

Finally, there is the contributing stage – beyond fourteen months. This is where the results need to begin to be delivered. Pressure mounts again – this time from the board. No excuses are available. The roller coaster is at the top of the hill and the leader is at the controls.

Know the timelines

It is interesting talking to leaders because they tend to have a very keen idea of the timelines which apply to their job and how their achievements will be measured.

Michael Critelli, chairman and former CEO of the Stamford, Connecticut-based, Pitney Bowes was asked about longevity in the CEO job. This was his reply: 'Ten to thirteen years for our size company is optimal. If I was running GE, twenty years may be optimal – but we're not that big. You keep the succession pipeline fresh. One of the risks of staying in the job for twenty years is that talented people who are a little younger and aspire to my job would leave. If they can have a reasonable tenure, I can keep them engaged and have a stronger team behind me. There is a benefit to having an orderly succession process and not staying until the board of directors forces you to leave. Beyond a certain length of time you get to believe that you can't be replaced so it is best to leave when you are still on top and still fresh.'

Critelli went on to reflect that a friend had told him that during the first three years on the job you're basically trying to get acclimatized. During the next five or six years you are a change agent – you put in place your programmes and vision for the company; and in the last four years you are focused on succession planning, ensuring the talent is there for the next generation.

Adding up to 100

Keeping these points in mind, let's consider the first 100 days and what a CEO needs to get done and, importantly, be seen to be doing. Of course, there are lots of other books which have their own suggestions. Some are more helpful – and humorous – than others. In their book *The Accidental Leader*, Harvey Robbins and Michael Finley offer an assessment test to establish how difficult the task ahead is. Answer the questions, add up the scores, and discover whether the challenge is: transition friendly; challenging but doable; uphill all the way; transition hostile; or Dilbertia. The first is encouraging, the last 'an insane enterprise whose true product is the spiritual evisceration of its people'.

There are, I think, six fundamental tasks for those first 100 days:

1 Mastering morale

2 Talking the talk

3 Assembling the team

4 Action!

5 Writing your own legend

6 Culture check and change

Mastering morale

'The reality in my company is that 30 per cent of the people do 100 per cent of the work. My job as CEO is to get the other 70 per cent to do something,' one CEO confided to me.

The morale of an organization's people is crucial at any time, but especially when a new leader takes over. In their book *The Enthusiastic Employee*, David Sirota, Louis Mischkind and Michael Meltzer found that the stock price of companies with high morale exceeds that of similar companies in the same industries by more than 2.5 to 1, and the stock price of companies with low morale lags behind their industry competitors by almost 5 to 1.

Testing an organization's morale is not difficult. Walk into any office and you will be able to detect morale levels fairly quickly. Within minutes you can identify those groups I pointed out earlier – the 20 per cent of people ready for change, the 60 per cent who are unsure, and the 20 per cent stubbornly adamant that change isn't for them. Organizations have enormous inbuilt political and cultural inertia.

Key to understanding and changing morale are a couple of points. First, people have a natural aspiration to be part of a winning team. The reality is that people don't move from job to job because of money – 60 per cent of people who have left organizations cite reasons other than money for their departure. People want meaningful, enjoyable and rewarding working lives. It is part of the CEO's job to convince people that their organization can meet their aspirations.

Second, in any organization there is good news. 'It is interesting how much a single leader can set in motion,' says Harvard Business School's Rosabeth Moss Kanter, who has studied turnarounds and the leadership skills required to make them happen. 'In turnarounds it is quite striking how much fresh leadership can accomplish by unlocking talent and potential which was already there in the organization but was stifled by rules, regulations and bureaucracy.' The CEO *is* the good news.

In any organization there are people who have exceptional skills, a track record of achievement; there are high-performing units, and so on. Even if the majority of the organization is filled with unexceptional people and poorly performing units with a track record of failure, there are bright lights. CEOs need to find them – and quick.

Getting to know people quickly is an art. This is corporate speed dating – like him, not him, she has promise, he is trying too hard to impress. For a senior executive or CEO, it could be through a speech to hundreds of employees. For a team leader it may be a chat with just a few team members. Either way it is essential to get it right.

Talking the talk

When I took over running the European and Asian operations of Heidrick & Struggles I distributed those colourful bands which people wear on their wrists to remind them of some worthy cause. Mine read: Fun/Respect. For any business leader this is the worthiest of worthy causes.

From the first day when I took over I was communicating my expectations and the direction I wanted to go. It was a matter of improving communication and letting people know I'm here,' says Monika Ribar. She committed herself to a lot of travelling to communicate her message and to get out and meet people. 'It's worth it because of the positive feedback and I'm learning so much. I always combine it with seeing customers, which, for me, is the only new part in my job because I have previously always managed people.'

Internally, Monika's key strategy meeting with the top management team laid the agenda clearly in front of them. 'I put the team together and aligned them under one roof and behind one target. It was a question of organization; setting the target, setting the agenda, for what we want to do; aligning them but also making them responsible. One weakness we identified is we didn't implement strategy. So I told the management team – I said, look, in a year's time if we are sitting again here and we are saying the same thing, we have a problem – all of us sitting here. Because nobody else will do it. It's our job to implement our strategy.'

I talked to Sam Parker, co-founder of media company MaxPitch Media, and he told me that one of the first things he did when he took over as CEO was to get rid of the instant messaging in the office. Everyone thought he was crazy. They said, how can you, a media Internet company, get rid of instant messaging? He said, because no one's talking to each other. It made a huge impact on the firm's culture.

To say communication is important to the new leader is a no-brainer. The question is how to communicate, both in term of style and medium. Authenticity is important. Communication should fit your personal style. Some leaders like to get personal, they are happy to open up and reveal aspects of their personal life. This offers the prospect of making an emotional connection. But it is also risky. Other leaders prefer to play safe, sticking primarily to business matters.

Other communications advice includes: communicating in a manner consistent with the corporate culture; choosing settings that a leader is comfortable is with – be it large crowds or small groups; consciously monitoring and adjusting the signals you are sending; reusing communications in various forums and formats to reinforce the message.

It is worth remembering that a new leader will not have all the answers. Asking questions and listening are important at this early stage. Don't restrict listening to insiders: try to get external perspectives, from customers and suppliers, for example.

Assembling the team

Assembling a strong team is right at the top of the 100 days to-do list. As Jim Collins said: 'First who, then what.' The idea that the leader comes in and picks a whole new team, is just that – an idea. The reality is that new leaders will have to work with the people they already have and get the best out of them. Certainly for the first 100 days.

New leaders must focus on getting to know people, and assessing strengths and weaknesses. They should probe to find out how well team members know their stuff. When team building think 'complementary' rather than 'supplementary'. A team of 'you' clones may be good for the ego but it's rarely good for the organization. The memory of the predecessor will linger, as will their values and actions. So new leaders should be careful not to badmouth them, or dismiss them, in front of the team. It risks alienating people loyal to the previous incumbent.

Finally, use the first team meetings to set the tone for those that follow. Set the style, the process.

Action!

Don't think vision, think priorities. Legendary CEO Lou Gerstner famously dismissed the vision-thing when he set out his course of action at IBM. Gerstner was the new CEO at an ailing IBM. His job? To breathe new life into a corporate giant on the critical list. It was normal practice for a CEO to spell out their vision. But Gerstner was right to resist the temptation. As he correctly observed at the time: 'The last thing IBM needs [now] is a vision.' Instead he set out five priorities to revive the company.

What were they? Stop haemorrhaging cash. Make sure the company is profitable by year two, inspiring confidence among the stakeholders. Implement a key customer strategy to demonstrate that the company has the interests of its customers at heart. Get redundancies out of the way quickly. Develop an intermediate strategy. Simply put, difficult to execute.

New leaders should look for some easy wins to set them on their way. Quick victories early on build credibility. Set out priorities, but don't list too many. Concentrate on a small, select few that are going to make a difference.

At Alliance Boots, Richard Baker identified three things he wanted to do: to become a successful international business; make a contribution to the healthcare industry; and make people proud to work for the company. 'They have actually remained very steady over the period I have been here,' he told me. 'I didn't build everything around them but I knew that was what success looked like.'

In addition, the new CEO needs to be inclusive. Drawing others into the strategy process is likely to lead to better buy-in. It is the same when encountering resistance. Roll with the punches, use them to your advantage, and if possible incorporate elements of resistance into the plan.

Writing your own legend

Change, it is commonly argued, begins with the CEO achieving some easy wins which signal that new rules now apply. In reality there are very few easy and meaningful things which a CEO can do to make an immediate material difference to the performance of the organization. But, what they can do is to create their own legend, to make it clear through symbolic acts what matters to them and the organization. News travels fast in organizations and it needs to work in the new CEO's favour. People gauge the health of the company by looking at the leader – the CEO is the weather vane for the whole organization.

For example, I heard of the CEO of a bank who was amazed to find that the approval process for certain loans involved a piece of paper being signed by someone on the first floor, then someone else on the third floor and then, finally, the CEO. All this took time as everyone who needed to sign was extremely busy and often not in the office. Loans took three days to approve. The next time the CEO received a loan approval document he called the other signatories into the office and told them that from now on one signature from either of them would suffice. Not rocket science, but the message was clear: customers come first and bureaucracy must be reduced. The story speedily spread through the bank.

At a telecommunications company the new CEO reassigned the parking spaces outside the entrance to customers rather than to senior executives. One of Greg Dyke's first actions as the new director general of the BBC was to get rid of the chauffeur-driven cars allocated to senior executives. It sent a clear message that cost cutting started at the top rather than the bottom of the organization.

'Executives sometimes think of things like changing the culture or getting good results from people as something that requires very elaborate, long programmes,' says Harvard Business School's Rosabeth Moss Kanter. 'But, someone like Greg Dyke at the BBC started with the behaviour of the eighteen people that reported to him. The quality of the way people treat each other starts with the team at the top.'

Culture check and change

Next on the new leader's agenda is transforming the culture of the organization, or environment, in which they are working.

'Culture isn't just one aspect of the game,' says Lou Gerstner; 'it is the game, in the end. And organization is nothing more than the collective capacity of its people to create value.'

To change culture first you have to know what you are dealing with. There may be words that are linked to the corporate culture. Words like excellence, shareholder value, integrity, and customer led. But in most companies the culture is revealed not through words but through actions. New leaders must read the unwritten code that the company lives by. They must interpret culture by observation and inquiry.

The actual transformation is something that the workforce does rather than the leader. The leader creates the conditions for change. They invite a culture change to take place. They do this by instituting new operating processes, by choosing a new management team, by leading by example.

Don't move too quickly though. Transforming a corporate culture takes time. Too much upheaval and something will give, and it may be the leader.

Mastering the 3 Rs

An interesting story about the early days comes from Chip McClure, chairman, CEO and president of ArvinMeritor. His approach was a good combination of listening, observing and decisive action. Chip was made CEO in August 2004. One of his initial aims was to spend time one-on-one with every board member. He travelled extensively around the world, listening and learning. 'I travelled to as many places as I could get to. I met with as many of our customers, suppliers and joint venture partners; visited our global plants and facilities, and talked to board members, our employees and shareholders. I also spent time on Wall Street – just listening,' he said.

Then came the action as Chip McClure rolled out his 3R strategy to rationalize and refocus the company. 'In these fast-paced times, you have to move quickly. The longer you go without doing something, the more you begin to create uncertainty. No matter what level you're at, people are looking for you to make decisions. And you have to do that with the information you've got at the time. You may have to tweak it a bit or go five degrees right or left, but you have to get out there. You cannot sit there and wait six, twelve, eighteen months to get something done. Are you fully knowledgeable on everything at that point? The answer is no, but after spending time listening, observing and learning you've got to go with the best you've got. And my clear advice to anybody, almost at any level, is take the first 90 or 100 days, and get out to as many places and meet with as many stakeholders as you can. Absorb the information and then identify a game plan and go forward. If you need to tweak it later, do it.'

This resulted in his three R strategy: rationalize, refocus and regenerate. The rationalization element came in the spring of 2005 when plant closures were announced. This restructuring initiative was necessary in order to rightsize the company. It was a $135 million restructuring programme involving eleven plants. Then came the refocus element. Over the next two years, the company focused on strengthening its core competences. The company was in too many different and non-core businesses. Therefore, it announced several divestitures. Its light vehicle aftermarket business was sold and then its emissions technology business. Next came the third R: regenerate. McClure and his team identified three key areas for growth.

Says Chip McClure: 'For the first couple of years, we were going to spend the majority of our time focusing on the first two Rs, which is exactly what we did. And now we're focused on the regeneration strategy. However, we are still continuing to rationalize or restructure our company. In the spring of 2007 we announced a second restructuring programme, which will take us to the next level. Change is a constant. As the industry continues to change, you can't just get locked into one thing and say, that's it for ever. You've got to be flexible and adapt quickly to the changes in the industry.' Think–act–change could be the new CEO's mantra.

Beware of isolation

Of course, there are many obstacles in the way. The biggest threat in the first 100 days – and beyond – is isolation. The CEO is often in a new industry with a new team. And everyone expects instant results. The potential for isolation is enormous. Being aware of this is crucially important.

'I didn't appreciate the problem of isolation,' Richard Baker of Alliance Boots told me. 'I needed a private advisory group of people I could talk to who would empathize and understand the issues I was dealing with. There are times when it is very complex and you really don't know what to do, so I built up this network of people. I talk to a businessman coach outside the company and in particular my father. You really need someone else to talk to.'

Ironically, perhaps the loneliest job in the world is when a CEO is brought in and the company founder is still in situ as chairman. Think of Phil Knight at Nike who brought in William Perez as CEO. Perez lasted a mere thirteen months. At Apple Computer in the 1980s, Steve Jobs recruited John Sculley to take the company on to the next level with his marketing experience at Pepsi. It didn't last. Founders like Ted Waitt of Gateway, Michael Dell and Charles Schwab have failed to resist the temptation to return as CEOs. There are many other examples of unpassed torches.

Whether they have a founding father looking over their shoulder or not, the CEO must invest time in building relationships with key influencers both inside and outside the organization. This may only be a handful of people, but they are the people whose views count in the organization and whose views can make or break a CEO's tenure.

Responses differ. Some CEOs will bring in someone they can trust to share the burden. Others take another route. When he took over as CEO of Ocean DHL, John Allen eschewed the option of bringing outsiders straight into the management team. He wanted to show that he thought the people in the organization were up to the job and to give them an opportunity to shine. This was a statement of faith, but not of blind faith. Later, he recruited an external CFO and COO.

Get lucky

There is one final element during the first 100 days and beyond. It is inexplicable and beyond management: luck. Napoleon hoped to recruit lucky generals and so, too, must organizations. CEOs have no control over the vicissitudes of global markets. The best CEOs maximize their influence over what matters to the organization and over the aspects of its performance they can influence. And then, hopefully, there is the added spice of good fortune.

Key points

> It really is tough at the top. Success must be built on first understanding the time frames of the process. This begins with anticipation and is followed by exploration, building and contributing. Only fools rush in without a keen idea of the process and its associated time frames.

> During the early stages there are six key things the new CEO must focus on:

1 Mastering morale – Take soundings on how people feel.

2 Talking the talk – Constantly and carefully communicate.

3 Assembling the team – Leadership is teamwork.

4 Action! – The job is about action; but focused, deliberate action is preferable to indiscriminately doing things for the sake of doing something.

5 Writing your own legend – Symbolic actions can shape your entire tenure.

6 Culture check and change – Any change must involve understanding and changing the corporate culture.

> Finally, beware isolation and wish for good fortune.

Resources

Bruch, Heike and Ghoshal, Sumantra, 'Management is the art of doing and getting done', *Business Strategy Review*, Autumn 2004.
Business Week, 'How to Take the Reins at Top Speed', 5 February, 2007.
Ciampa, Dan and Watkins, Michael, *Right From the Start*, Harvard Business School Press, 1999.
Gerstner, Lou, *Who Says Elephants Can't Dance?*, Collins, 2002.

Kanter, Rosabeth Moss, *Confidence*, Harvard Business School Press, 2006.

Robbins, Harvey and Finley, Michael, *The Accidental Leader*, Jossey-Bass, 2003.

Sirota, David, Mischkind, Louis and Meltzer, Michael, *The Enthusiastic Employee*, Wharton Publishing, 2005.

Trapp, Roger, 'Turnarounds – a turn for the better', *Financial Director*, 23 May 2005.

Watkins, Michael, *The First 90 Days*, Harvard Business School Press, 2003.

Chapter **3**

The job
Leadership, strategy and execution

The CEO's job begins with leadership. The CEO is in charge. But where are they leading their people and how can they ensure they get there? Without strategy and execution leadership is decorative.

You don't become a leader without followers.
You only know if you have followers when you ask
them to do something really difficult and they do it
with enthusiasm.

Richard Baker, CEO, Alliance Boots

Who's in charge?

Gerry Roche, senior chairman of Heidrick & Struggles, tells the story of how he was brought in by Bill Pailey who founded the CBS Corporation and turned it into what was known as the Tiffany Network, the best of the networks. It was the leading broadcasting organization in the world at the time and Pailey was the equivalent of Rupert Murdoch. Gerry was brought in to find Pailey's successor. After the company had gone public the board had leant on Pailey to bring in a chief operating officer as the anointed successor. Gerry recruited someone called Tom Wyman, who was the chairman and CEO of Green Giant in the Mid-West. Wyman was an extraordinarily impressive candidate. 'He looked like Gary Cooper, just the quintessence of the top CEO – he'd sit on the cover of *Fortune* beautifully,' Gerry recalls.

When Tom Wyman was interviewed by Pailey he thought he was perfect and said, okay, let's make him an offer. The trouble was that Pailey had a record of hiring COOs for a year or two and then firing them. So, Tom Wyman told Gerry that he wouldn't touch the job unless Pailey were to make him CEO. 'I went back to Pailey, this huge man with his huge ego and a huge reputation and I told him that Tom Wyman wouldn't come unless Pailey made him CEO. And he said, "COO, CEO, who gives a damn as long as everybody knows who's boss around here."'

Gerry recounts this story for a simple reason. He explains: 'You can take titles and play with them and you can take "non-executive directors" and you can take "chairman" and you can say "executive chairman" – and my title now is senior chairman – and you can play with titles and structures, but the fundamental question is who's running the show? And that's the definition in my book of the CEO: the person who is responsible for the successful running of the operation. That includes everything. That's what the CEO is responsible for: the strategy, the execution, the hiring of people, the legal function, the HR function and, to the extent that he designs the structure under him, where he divides it into operations and support and public exposure jobs. I have difficulty coming up with some nice McKinsey or Harvard definition for the job description of a CEO. The bottom line is the CEO is the person who's responsible to the shareholders for running the firm, and he is responsible to the board of directors who are responsible for picking the CEO. It's that simple.'

Actually leading a business isn't about a job title, a large office or a parking space. When he took over as CEO of Alliance Boots, Richard Baker moved into an open plan office rather than the traditional CEO's office. 'Businesses are run by teams and I have a team of 100,000. I may have the captain's armband on but I am like everyone else.

'I don't need a lot of status. Too much status means that people won't talk to you,' he says. On his first day, Richard was given a name badge like all the company's employees. It said 'Mr R.A. Baker, Chief Executive'. He asked for it to be changed simply to 'Richard.'

Inventing the CEO

The strange thing is that, going back forty years no one had heard of the CEO. Sure, the concept of the CEO existed, as did that of the executive board, but the person we now call the CEO went by a different title.

Companies had presidents, vice presidents and chairmen. *The Men Who Are Making America*, published in 1917 by Forbes magazine, is chock full of the corporate titans of the day, people like J.P. Morgan, Cyrus McCormick, F.W. Woolworth and Henry Ford. Yet among the roll-call of famous names, and tales of corporate derring-do, there is not a mention of the CEO.

We have the *Harvard Business Review* to thank for thrusting the title of CEO into the business consciousness. The title 'CEO' cropped up increasingly during the mid-1970s at a time when managers were getting to grips with new management techniques such as quality control and SWOT analysis.

Harold Klein, associate professor of general and strategic management at the Fox School of Business, Temple University, Philadelphia, suggests a reason for the proliferation of the CEO tag. The captains of industry in post-war America were keen to step down from running their corporations, but less keen to give up the title of president. So, instead, the title of CEO was created. The presidents retained their title but passed the day-to-day running of the organization to the CEO.

Over time this shift in responsibility devalued the title of president to the point where the president reported to the CEO, and now is often titled chief operating officer.

The objectives

So, that's how the job evolved. But what are CEOs expected to achieve? What are the key performance measures for a CEO? There are many opinions on this. 'The bigger the company is, the more the job is really managing the people, putting the right people at the right place, thinking about the future of the company, trying to bring everything under one roof, setting the strategy,' says Monika Ribar of Panalpina.

For me, there are three key things which keep employees happy, engaged and loyal to the company and these constitute the underlying objectives in everything that I do. They are:

1 Interest in what they do – be it marketing, finance, consulting, or whatever.

2 Compensation – not just what people are paid and their bonuses but treating people fairly.

3 Learning – when candidates approach us as a search firm it is usually because they feel they have stopped learning and developing in their current firm.

Increasingly, as my colleagues and I look for the CEOs of the future we find ourselves coming back to that third point – learning – as the most critical. Generation Y – those born between 1977 and 2005 – will have an average of fourteen jobs by the time they are 38. It seems to me that the organizations which are going to succeed in the long term are those which provide their employees with the right learning opportunities. As a leader I hope I never stop learning, and when I'm promoting people or looking for future leaders within my firm, I look closely at how they encourage, develop and train the talent below them. There are few more effective tests of leadership potential.

According to leadership thinker Warren Bennis, the key performance indicators are:

1 Is there alignment of the organization? Which means is there a collectively shared definition of success that's understood throughout the organization – and rewarded throughout the organization?

2 Is there adaptive capacity? In other words, is there resilience? Is there the sense of being able to foresee and adapt to continual change – without the habit of success getting in the way. There's a great line in Samuel Beckett's play *Waiting for Godot*, where Didi, one of the two tramps, says to the other tramp Gogo: 'Habit is a great deadener.' Successful habits are even more of a deadener.

3 Financial results – however measured. Whether it's market capitalization; or return on investment; whether it's looking at the success or lack of success of acquisitions or divestitures – whatever the company is using as its measure of financial success has to be taken into account.

4 Does the organization develop a bench – a cadre – of future leaders? Is there mentoring going on?

5 Does the workforce feel motivated, empowered, animated and engaged?

6 Transparency. Is the organization relatively open?

7 To what extent are resources being put into future research and development?

Beyond charisma

There's not a lot you can argue with in Bennis's summary. The CEO's job description is incredibly varied and demanding. Most jobs come with a job description, a lengthy list of the exact parameters of responsibility. But when you reach the top, the job descriptions abruptly end. You are chief executive officer, a phrase as riddled with ambiguity as it is resonant with corporate status. You are left alone to make it up as you go along.

The loneliness can be hard: you wake up and realize you have become the person you used to complain about. Compared with the experience of most executives, the CEO has enormous freedom – to choose what to do and when and with whom. Previously I had been an executive cocooned in routine and certainty; as CEO I realized uncertainty rules.

Phil Hodgson, co-author of *Relax, It's Only Uncertainty*, sees the CEO's lack of control as the greatest challenge. 'The CEO faces uncertainty outside the organization in the form of expectations about organizational performance, direction and, if appropriate, stock price. But also faces uncertainty inside the organization in the form of managerial performance, operational effectiveness and realization of human potential,' he says. 'The role of the CEO is therefore to choose the areas of uncertainty where the strategic challenges will be met externally, and support the areas of learning where the managerial challenges will be met internally.'

CEOs have to learn to revel in the uncertainty, the ambiguity offered by the job. 'Management is a science, but being a CEO is an art,' former Toshiba CEO Taizo Nishimura once reflected.

And the CEO has to be an artist of every medium. 'I think the CEO has three jobs, or roles,' says Barry Gibbons, former chairman and CEO of Burger King and now an author and consultant. 'First, to have "The Dream" (this is *not* a mission, or a mission statement). It is Bill Gates seeing a PC on every table. Second, the CEO is all about *how* you do business, less about what you do. The style factors. What do you stand for? What do you stand by? What are the imperatives? What's the balance of the company? Are you responsive or deaf? Backbone or invertebrate? Third, the CEO is the leader figure – and watched by a whole range of audiences. This is not about style versus substance, it's about understanding how you *personally* can best impact the first two roles. What are the key audiences – Wall

Street? Consumers? Lobby groups? Your employees? Unions? Get involved personally and show them what you and the company stand for.'

Jacques Aigrain, CEO of Swiss Re, offered another take on the role. Swiss Re is the world's biggest reinsurance group. When I spoke to Jacques, Swiss Re's profits had just doubled and its net income stood at CHF 4.6 billion ($3.8 billion, €2.7 billion). Jacques took over as CEO early in 2006, after a spell as deputy CEO. He started his career with JP Morgan in 1981. 'A large majority of people don't really understand what a CEO does. Even within your own company most people do not know how the CEO's time is spent,' he says. 'In my case, in the first year I had a huge number of tactical issues to deal with, then the more time that has passed the more I'm looking forward to see what the strategy should be, what the key challenges are in the longer term.'

The one-word job description

If you could pick one word to sum up the CEO's job it is this: *leadership*.

Now, leadership can become confused with charisma. In the New Testament 'charisms' were gifts bestowed by Holy Spirit. People with charisma in this sense include good leaders, but they are also those with the ability to perform miracles or speak in tongues. Often we expect CEOs to perform miracles and sometimes they speak in tongues.

Charismatic leaders loom large in history. They include Napoleon, Churchill and Gandhi. In more recent times charisma has become synonymous with secular success. 'Charisma wasn't always important in business,' notes Rakesh Khurana, an associate professor at Harvard Business School. 'For three decades following World War II, the typical chief executive was an organization man who worked his way up the ranks.'

According to Professor Khurana, that started to change in 1979 with the appointment of Lee Iacocca as CEO of Chrysler. 'Iacocca was inspirational in a way that previous business leaders had not been. His successful turn-around of Chrysler made him a national hero in America and ushered in the era of the charismatic CEO.'

Jack Welch at GE, Steve Jobs at Apple Computer, and Virgin's Richard Branson are all examples of charismatic business leaders. They radiate a personal magnetism that attracts employees and customers alike. But how much of that aura comes from their position as leader?

A lot, according to Professor Manfred Kets de Vries, of INSEAD. 'It's a fantasy', he says. 'People project their expectations on to the leader. But if you want to stimulate a fantasy you can do a few things. It helps if you are a good orator. It helps if you can tell stories, and use imagery. It helps if you have a good memory for names. It helps if you are attentive and people at least have the illusion that you listen to them – what I call the teddy bear factor. It also helps if you are willing to ask questions and challenge the status quo.'

Charismatic leaders also rely on symbol manipulation. In ancient times leaders often wore special clothing, masks and ornaments to appear larger than life, notes Professor Khurana. Kings and queens assume charisma through their family heritage. For the modern business leader, private jets, limousines, palatial homes and the other trappings of corporate power perform the same function.

At this point the dangers of charisma become apparent. There is a darker side. Bernie Ebbers at WorldCom and Dennis Kozlowski at Tyco were both charismatic leaders. The collapse of Enron was also fuelled by a heady cocktail of charisma and greed. Right up until the very end, former CEO Jeffrey Skilling and CFO Andrew Fastow, continued to charm investors and analysts at gatherings that one insider likened to revival meetings.

The point is that charisma can blind people to the failings of an individual or their arguments. This is causing a reappraisal among leadership experts. Jeffrey Garten, dean of the Yale School of Management and author of *The Politics of Fortune: A New Agenda for Business Leadership*, for example, argues that an important task for today's leaders is to redefine the character of leadership. 'Much of the past decade was about the swaggering and self-promoting CEO,' he notes, 'but it would be a misreading of current and future requirements if business leaders concluded that charisma is a bad thing. Indeed, it is a trait that is part and parcel of effective leadership at any time.'

So, the first thing to be said is that charisma is not the be-all and end-all of leadership. I know plenty of CEOs who are not charismatic, but they are certainly leaders.

Interestingly, too, even if you can get one, celebrity CEOs do not always add value. Jack Welch, Steve Jobs, Louis Gerstner, Bill Gates, Larry Ellison, Andrew Grove and Carly Fiorina are just some of the CEOs (and former CEOs) who have had celebrity status conferred on them by the business media. Interestingly, many CEOs I talk to are uncomfortable with this trend. They don't want to be celebrities; they want to run great organizations. 'There is a worrying trend of celebratization. Business reporting is much more personalized. There are fewer stories about companies. People have very unrealistic expectations of CEOs,' laments Richard Baker.

The question must be what impact 'star' CEOs actually have. Four business researchers examined the results of the *Financial World* 'CEO of the Year' contest between 1992 and 1997 to see whether they or their companies benefited from their fame. The study covered 278 companies from the

S&P 500, collecting data on total CEO compensation and company performance – both changes in share price in the days immediately after the rankings were published and market returns (total change in share price for the year). They then tested the sample to see the effect of CEO star status, comparing how the firms with celebrity leaders performed against the average stock market performance and, more specifically, against market expectations for that firm.

The findings showed an initial positive effect for the organization. For the firm, there was an immediate uptick in share price following the announcement of the winners of the CEO contest. This leads to a slight rise in market return – both against the average and the individual expectation – which is most pronounced the day after the results are announced (up about 0.25 per cent). But this effect soon faded as the information was integrated into investors' evaluation of the firm, contributing to higher expectations of those firms led by star CEOs. Compared with these elevated hopes, the results quickly turned negative. Within thirty days the effect on expected market return for the firm versus actual market return became marginally negative, and over eight months it became significantly negative.

Meanwhile, the CEO benefits over both the short and the long term. 'Winning a medal in the current year increases a CEO's pay by approximately 10 per cent,' the authors note, 'and each medal awarded in the previous five years adds almost 5 per cent to his/her pay.'

The findings suggest that boards expect higher performance from their star CEOs and reward them accordingly. Similarly, analysts expect star CEOs to deliver superior results to those of their less famous peers and raise their hopes. But there is no clear evidence that their confidence is justified. In fact, firm performance often fails to live up to these higher expectations. So, even though the celebrity CEOs may not perform any better or any worse than average, their celebrity status means that they are rewarded with above-average compensation (compared with non-winning CEOs). This suggests that paying over-the-odds compensation to attract star CEOs is a risky strategy.

So if celebrity is not a useful measure of CEO efficacy, what is?

The meaning of leadership

CEOs are usually judged on financial results. But, there is another equally important aspect of leadership: providing meaning.

Research by Joel Podolny, Novartis Professor of Leadership and Management, Rakesh Khurana, an associate professor; and Marya Hill-Popper, a doctoral student at Harvard Business School, suggests that leadership impacts on meaning in several ways. First, leaders make architectural choices – how to structure the organization, design jobs, and allocate roles and responsibilities – that shape how people who work in the organization experience their jobs. Second, leaders engage in symbolic actions – through the stories they tell, the symbols and rituals they create, and other highly visible actions. The leader is both architect and visionary, and both roles impact on the meaning that individuals experience through work.

So what is the connection between meaning-making capacity and economic performance? Podolny and his co-authors offer two answers. The first, as they admit, is a defiant one. 'One of the most significant problems with the study of organizations is that the concern with economic outcomes has trumped the concern with other outcomes. Satisfaction, meaning, social welfare – all seem to be regarded as of secondary importance.'

They do not believe that establishing a connection is essential. Rather, they assert that the meaningfulness of actions is important enough in its own right to not have to justify a focus on meaning by establishing a connection with economic performance.

But they also acknowledge that this is not an entirely satisfactory answer. Even if one accepts that meaning is of paramount importance, it cannot be sustained to the complete exclusion of a focus on performance – because the organization will not survive.

Nor should we assume that causality flows entirely from meaning to performance. Just as it is reasonable to assume that individuals perform better when they find their work more meaningful, it could be that better economic performance has a positive impact on the meaning individuals derive from their work. Even if we ultimately find that meaning creation does not have a significant impact on performance, Podolny et al. maintain that greater attention should be given to meaning. Meaning creation, in other words, is too important to be subordinated to economic performance.

Conclusion? 'Meaning creation is an important phenomenon regardless of its relation to economic performance. Indeed, we can think of no other phenomenon that is more worthy of explanation,' say the Harvard experts.

For business leaders, providing meaning is as important as impacting on performance.

The magical ingredients

The amazing thing when you look at leadership (and plenty of people have – witness the 2,000-plus books on leadership published every year) is that the ingredients which go to make up effective leadership remain elusive. 'A leader is a dealer in hope,' Napoleon once observed.

Current thinking on leadership reflects recent experience. In particular, there is widespread discontent with a particular sort of heroic (or narcissistic) leadership – which many believe contributed to such corporate scandals as Enron, Tyco and Vivendi.

Looked at more positively, what do I consider the essential ingredients for leadership?

First, any leader is only as good as their followers. I heard a story about the CEO of an international chain of hotels. His measure of success was whether the maid cleaning a room in one of the chain's furthest outposts would neatly turn up the toilet paper. It is a very small thing to consider in a huge international operation, but it is built around realizing that if the CEO is doing their job well then it is having an impact on everyone in the organization.

When I spoke with H. Patrick Swygert he was president of Howard University, a job he had held since 1995. Soon after, he announced his intention to leave the post in June 2008. Patrick studied law at Howard and was previously president at the University of Albany. Along the way he has taught throughout the world and is on the board of Fannie Mae, United Technologies, the Hartford Financial Services Group and is on the CIA's External Advisory Board.

'You can be a great leader, or at least have the attributes of a great leader, and have no followers,' Patrick observed. 'How often have we seen people who, at least on paper, fit the profile, but they just can't get people to work and walk with them. I would say that comes about for two reasons. One, some believe they can act without the advice or input of others. They believe they know everything or know as much, or more, than anyone in the room. They tend to only half listen and people pick up on that very, very quickly.

'Second, there are some people who don't have that kind of all-encompassing, far-reaching intelligence, but they're intelligent in one way, but not intelligent enough to let other people have something to say, and a piece of the outcome. I think that's one of the reasons why some, otherwise brilliant people, can't do anything but lead themselves to the rest rooms.' (On a similar theme, one amazed new CEO told me, 'People do actually follow you to the bathroom.')

Quiet leadership

The second key to understanding leadership is that humility outperforms charisma. In his book, *Good to Great,* Jim Collins examines how a good company becomes an exceptional company. The book introduces a new term to the leadership lexicon: Level 5 leadership. Level 5 refers to the highest level in a hierarchy of executive capabilities. Leaders at the other four levels may be successful but they are unable to elevate companies from mediocrity to sustained excellence.

Level 5 leadership challenges the assumption that transforming companies from good to great requires larger-than-life leaders. The leaders that came out on top in Collins's five-year study were relatively unknown outside their industries. The findings appear to signal a shift of emphasis away from the hero to the anti-hero. According to Collins, humility is a key ingredient of Level 5 leadership. His simple formula is Humility + Will = Level 5. 'The central dimension for Level 5 is a leader who is ambitious first and foremost for the cause, for the company, for the work, not for himself or herself; and has an absolutely terrifying iron will to make good on that ambition,' says Collins. 'It is that combination, the fact that it's not about them, it's not first and foremost for them, it's for the company and its long-term interests, of which they are just a part. But it's not a meekness; it's not a weakness; it's not a wallflower type. It's the other side of the coin.'

Balancing IQ and EQ

Third, leadership requires sensitivity. Dan Goleman's book *The New Leaders* (entitled *Primal Leadership* in America), makes the case for cultivating emotionally intelligent leaders. In it, Goleman and co-authors Richard E. Boyatzis and Annie McKee, explore how the four domains of emotional intelligence – self-awareness, self-management, social awareness and relationship management – give rise to different styles of leadership. These constitute a leadership repertoire, which enlightened leaders can master to maximize their effectiveness.

My belief is that, at the heart of the CEO's job and integral to leadership is the ability to balance IQ and EQ (emotional quotient). CEOs now require a broad spectrum of knowledge. The best CEOs are adept at applying their analytical skills and their emotional skills at the right times. They aren't purely people people, but can make sense of complex market data and strategic plans. The important thing is that they are able to balance the two elements.

'You can't be a dictator or someone who listens to everyone,' reflects Michael Critelli, chairman of Pitney Bowes. 'You have to balance stakeholders and make independent judgements. People put you in the job to represent the collective will of the organization not to respond to every fad and fashion of the moment.'

Another CEO I talked to put it like this: 'The problem is that you think that everyone thinks like you. But if they thought like you, they wouldn't need you as CEO.'

The need for balance is emphasized by Rob Goffee and Gareth Jones, two professors at London Business School, in their book *Why Should Anyone Be Led By You?* Goffee and Jones argue that effective leaders consciously move between being close to and distant from the people they lead. 'The leader's job is to look out for all the stakeholders in an organization, and that can't be done if the leader is too close to any one group of them. Mired in a complex situation, the leader must rise above it to understand it. Preserving distance may be the only way to see the full picture,' they say. 'When establishing goals, objectives, and the rules of the game distance is essential. Norms, values and standards need to be communicated as non-negotiable. These are the bedrock on which operations are built. This can only be done effectively early in a leadership relationship, with as much distance and formality as possible.'

Of course, as Goffee and Jones point out, distance can sometimes be overdone. As director general of the BBC, John Birt was renowned for his distance: so much so that when he announced a major reorganization it came as news to everyone except the board and the team of consultants who had come up with the plan. Contrast this approach with that of Birt's successor, Greg Dyke, who was a master of closeness. Successful CEOs flit easily and consciously between the two modes.

Vision and strategy

'I was in the navy for some time. On the bridge of a ship you've got the captain, then you have the executive officer, who is the second in command. The captain decides where we're going, what ports we have to make, what part of the battle plan we're going to be in, what part of the fleet we're in and where we are going. The executive officer is the guy that he turns to and says, all right, now get this damn ship there and do what's been planned,' says Gerry Roche. 'You have to boil this down to its simplest elements. Two functions are performed in every corporation: planning and doing, or vision and execution. The talents for doing those jobs, in general, are not the same. The idea that the COO's job is the natural path to becoming CEO is often assumed but is not always the case. Skills for doing and executing are not always found, nor do they necessarily lead to skills in vision and planning. Special attention needs to be given to the danger that this unwarranted assumption could lead to putting the wrong person in the

CEO role. Executives who do both well do indeed exist. But they are rare and ultimately the real stars in succession planning.'

I think we can all pretty much accept that leadership is at the core of being a CEO. The next two elements are a little bit more complicated because they tend not to be evident in the same person. They are, an ability to create strategy and an ability to execute. As Gerry points out, you are asking a lot of any CEO to be able both to dream and to deliver.

But that is what they have to do. While the COO takes care of the operational nitty-gritty, it is the CEO's job to create and implement a vision and strategy, the desired destination. 'The CEO must have a vision. The business environment is going to change over the next five to ten years, and they need to communicate that to their people. Preparing for the future now is a key role for the CEO,' says Seung-Yu Kim, CEO of Hana Financial Group.

'The chief executive', says Karan Bilimoria, founder of Cobra beer, 'has got to have a vision, to display a certain confidence to show that they are somebody who is looking ahead, who knows where they are going and where the company is going, and they have that confidence and the faith that inspires others to go with them on that journey.'

Change begins with a vision. It has to. 'You cannot make a change or even engage in a process of change if at the beginning you do not know where you want to go. Establishing the destination, establishing the purpose is fundamental. If you do not have a purpose, do not even try to make any changes, because they will fail. Having from the beginning a clear vision, a clear sense of purpose, is fundamental to any change,' Carlos Ghosn told me. 'Up to 1999, Nissan was a company in disarray. Company objectives were set and people worked hard to achieve them, but then the course kept changing. People lost a sense of motivation and did not know where to go. When I came on board in 1999, my sole objective was very simple: it was to revive Nissan. This objective would determine all our priorities. It would determine even the people we would count on to achieve them. In 1999, we had to revive the company. There would be no compromises and no half-measures. Nothing that could threaten the revival of the company would be accepted.

'What was true then is still true today. If you do not have a shared and attractive destination, you can forget about any process of change.'

Many CEOs spend their first 100 days, or longer, cogitating on what the vision and strategy might be. This is – or can be – incredibly valuable for the CEO and the long-term health of the organization.

'During the first 100 days people doubted my ideas. But, after talking to a lot of people, after 100 days, I created my vision. People doubted that it could be done. People didn't believe me. But, talking about the same things, consistently over three years ago, people started to believe. And now what's happening is in line with my vision. Sometimes you have to change implementation depending on the competitive situation. But having a very simple vision and very consistent message is important. Perhaps people thought I'm stupid because I was always saying the same things, but, in a sense, I wanted to brainwash people,' says Takeshi Niinami, CEO of Lawson.

Patrick Swygert identifies the failure to come up with a vision as a characteristic of those who fail to make the leap to truly significant leadership. 'One reason why otherwise ostensibly great leaders, at least in terms of credentials and stature, are unable to lead is because they are unable either to articulate or to fashion a vision, a sense of purpose that people really can rally around. They may know where they're going, but they can't quite get it over to other people.'

Execution

And then it has to happen. Execution is central to the CEO's job.

You might think that the capacity to act positively and purposefully is obvious. It is, but it is equally rare. Research by Heike Bruch and Sumantra Ghoshal found that only 10 per cent of executives fall into the category of being full of purposeful action. Of the rest, two-fifths fall into the category of 'distracted managers'. Full of energy and highly motivated they may be, but they also rapidly switch from one activity to another, an activity described as firefighting. They spend their days flitting from meeting to meeting not knowing what they want to make happen. They're too busy to see problems coming up.

Firefighting lacks any strategic imperative and consequently distracted managers are unable to lead others. This wouldn't be so bad if it wasn't for that fact that so many organizations have cultures that support this type of behaviour. Strategy guru Henry Mintzberg spent time analysing senior executives at work. He found that managers were slaves to the moment, moving from task to task with every move dogged by another diversion, another telephone call. The median time spent on any one issue was a mere nine minutes. (As Mintzberg's work was published in 1973 it would be safe to conclude that this figure has probably been significantly reduced thanks to email, mobile phones and much more.)

I have learnt the need to separate what is urgent versus what is important; and that comes down to judgement. My years in executive search have shown me that the leaders who fail are those who micro-manage and overcomplicate everything. Those leaders who are convinced they must be involved in every detail. I am curious about everything but realize I cannot be an expert in every single area of our business and I have to rely on the expertise of others. If you have the right people in place then this is not hard because you trust those people to tell you what is crucial; and they grow and develop because they know they have your support – we all know how good it feels to be relied on.

Another 30 per cent of executives are procrastinators. 'They can't even get started,' says Bruch. 'Experience has taught them that whatever they do won't make any difference to anything. They certainly can't motivate others.' And then there are the disengaged (about 20 per cent). These people are focused, but not driven or excited by what they do. They lack the energy to deal with problems or to drive things through.

The problem is that many managers confuse being active with being productive. They become too absorbed with routine tasks and firefighting, leaving little time or energy for issues requiring reflection, systematic planning or creative thinking. One CEO I talked to kept Friday clear in his diary so he could deal with the things which emerged during the week or even, unusually, to get ahead. It worked for him.

'Action demands energy,' explains Professor Bruch. 'Some managers fail to take purposeful action simply because they lack energy. Some are exhausted or burnt out from stress and do not have the inner resources to re-energize themselves. For others, the lack of energy may be relevant to a particular project which is not meaningful to them. Without energy, they are unable to "go the extra mile" that is often necessary to accomplish non-routine tasks.' Focus, on the other hand, involves concentrated attention, she says. 'It is the ability to zero in on a goal and see it successfully through to completion.'

Key points

> The CEO's job description is the subject of continuing debate. But, all agree that it is wide ranging. At its heart lies leadership.

> The contemporary practice of leadership has moved on from the historical command-and-control model. Leadership is not solely about charisma – though being charismatic helps. Instead it needs to be based on understanding the needs of followers; humility rather than ego; and being able to balance EQ and IQ.

> CEOs must also master execution, purposeful action. Their actions must be carefully focused and their energies channelled into acting at the right time in the right way.

> CEOs are also responsible for generating and living the company's vision and for creating and implementing strategy.

Resources

Badaracco, J., Jr, 'We don't need another hero', *Harvard Business Review*, September 2001.

Bennis, Warren, 'The seven ages of the leader', *Harvard Business Review*, January 2004.

Bilimoria, Karan, *Bottled for Business*, Capstone Press, 2007.

Bruch, Heike and Ghoshal, Sumantra, 'Management is the art of doing and getting done', *Business Strategy Review*, Autumn 2004.

Collins, James, 'Level 5 leadership: the triumph of humility and fierce resolve', *Harvard Business Review*, January 2001.

Collins, Jim, *Good to Great,* HarperBusiness, 2001.

Collins, Jim and Porras, Jerry I., *Built to Last: Successful Habits of Visionary Companies*, HarperBusiness, 1995.

Conger, Jay and Kanungo, Rabindra, *Charismatic Leadership in Organisations*, Sage, 1998.

Dearlove, Des, 'Leading from the Top: An Interview with Warren Bennis', EFMD Thought Leader Series, efmd.org.

Dvorak, John C., 'Too many chiefs', *PC Magazine* October, 2002.

Garten, Jeffrey, *The Politics of Fortune: A New Agenda for Business Leadership*, Harvard Business School Press, 2002.

Goffee, Rob and Jones, Gareth, 'Why should anyone be led by you?', *Harvard Business Review,* October/November, 2000.

Goffee, Rob and Jones, Gareth, *Why Should Anyone Be Led By You?*, Harvard Business School Press, 2006.

Goleman, Daniel, *Emotional Intelligence*, Bantam, 1995.

Goleman, Daniel and Boyatzis, Richard, *Primal Leadership*, Harvard Business School Press, 2002.

Hodgson, Phil and White, Randall P., *Relax, It's Only Uncertainty*, FT Prentice Hall, 2004.

Mintzberg, Henry, *The Nature of Managerial Work*, Harper & Row, 1973.

Podolny, Joel, Khurana, Rhakesh and Hill-Popper, Marya, 'Revisiting the meaning of leadership', *Research in Organizational Behavior*, 26 (2005): 1–37.

PricewaterhouseCoopers, *9th Annual Global CEO Survey*, 2006.

Chapter **4**

The job

Communication and people

How do you convince people that you are the person to provide leadership, that your strategy is the right one and that execution relies on everyone contributing? Only connect.

A CEO has to be curious. What is going on? If you just sit in your office, I don't think that you can do the job like that and I don't think that you can do it in future.

Monika Ribar, CEO, Panalpina

Constantly communicating

'CEOs often fail not because of lack of strategic thinking but a lack of coherent thought about implementation and mobilizing the organization,' says Gurnek Bains, managing director of the business psychology consultancy YSC and one of the authors of *Meaning, Inc.* 'It really is about people. Before being CEOs managers usually understand this intellectually, but only when they actually do the job do they tend to understand it emotionally. Typically CEOs spend 40 to 50 per cent of their time communicating with people. They also spend a surprising amount of time thinking about the top talent in the company, building teams and attracting talented people.'

Gerry Roche, senior chairman at Heidrick & Struggles, is equally clear: 'The very definition of management is getting good work from others, not doing it yourself. How can you get work done through others if you aren't a good communicator or if you don't have good human sensitivities? Those are the two skills that ring my bell. Whether it's COO or CEO, you are not going to be measured on what you do yourself; you are going to be judged on the team that you build, enthuse, motivate, integrate, assess, compensate; you are going to be measured on what that team does. And what it takes to build and run a team is mainly communicating skills, human sensitivity, a bias for action and good judgement.'

If leadership is the job of the CEO, making this happen demands communication. CEOs constantly communicate; they connect authentically, powerfully and persuasively with people. At Heidrick & Struggles we produced a book of parables called *Listen.* There is one page that I like particularly which many of our consultants have framed on their office walls. It reads: 'As a partner and consultant you should follow your biological set up. Two ears and one mouth means listen twice as much as you talk.' I think that's a pretty good maxim for a CEO.

The reality is that better communications could – and perhaps should – sort out most of the day-to-day problems in organizations. Poor communication is the consistent downfall of organizations – now and tomorrow. Effective CEOs constantly communicate. Indeed, they often communicate exactly the same message but to different audiences. An appetite for repetition is part of the CEO's job description. And the repetition needs to be consistent, for there is danger in varying the message, even slightly, for different audiences. If we send a message to our employees in one region, the global grapevine immediately kicks in and soon it is all over the company: the message must be the same for all.

The need to communicate is particularly acute in troubled times. But it is a constant feature of the CEO's job – no matter what stage they are at.

Asked about how he spent his time as CEO, Pitney Bowes' Michael Critelli estimated that around 5 per cent was spent on board and corporate governance matters; 25–30 per cent on meetings – individually with people who worked with him, staff meetings and around 150 one-to-one meetings every year with people from all levels of the organization; 5–10 per cent meeting with industry officials, politicians and other regulators; and 10–15 per cent in some form of interaction with customers. In addition, he attributed around five days a year to talking to shareholders, analysts and rating agencies and his remaining time is spent on a variety of outside activities which somehow relate to his job. Whatever the split, it is clear that communicating with people inside and outside the organization lies at the heart of the CEO's job description.

Wire-less

An interesting approach to communication comes from Richard Baker, CEO of Alliance Books. He admits to being 'very selfish' in the communication media he uses. He doesn't use email ('too slow and one-dimensional') or possess a BlackBerry. (A number of other CEOs are strongly anti-BlackBerry – 'I'm not a big email person. I don't have a BlackBerry. And I don't want to have a BlackBerry,' says Monika Ribar of Panalpina.)

Richard Baker rarely writes a memo. Instead he sends a lot of text messages – around 25 a day – and is constantly talking to people. 'If someone has a problem, they send me a text, we talk and the problem gets solved. I have lots of short telephone calls. Talking is a two-way dialogue so you learn much. If someone says it is urgent, I respond immediately. This is especially important in a newly merged company.'

The day we spoke, Richard had begun the day by calling one of his store managers whose store had just broken a record. Imagine the motivational impact of having the CEO on the line. His second call had been to someone who had written to him with a few ideas having read an article about the company. None of this is eye catching or headline making, but it is incredibly powerful in forging your own legend within the organization and in learning about what is really going on.

I haven't abandoned my BlackBerry but have learnt how to use it to my advantage – I use it as an alarm, to keep an eye on what is going on. I only respond if it is something critical – something that needs my input quickly and directly or arbitrating between a number of different parties to keep a process moving quickly. I have no compunction about switching my BlackBerry off on the weekend and when I am doing something else. I was talking to an executive and he told me about getting into bed one night with his BlackBerry – his wife turned to him and said, 'Only one of us is staying in this bed tonight.'

Face time

One of the most striking examples of communication I have come across comes from Seung-Yu Kim of Korea's Hana Financial Group. His willingness to open up communication channels with employees is deeply impressive. 'My people can send me emails at any time, even very early in the morning, two or three o'clock. They really appreciate it and that's why they try to listen to me.' At the company's training centre, training finishes at nine or ten o'clock in the evening. Seung-Yu Kim makes a point of taking the opportunity to talk to the groups of thirty or forty people. 'I talk with them personally and meet face-to-face with the people. And then I accompany them to one of the nearby small bars and drink Korean liquor, *soju*. Actually I don't drink at all, so sometimes I drink water because the colour is the same! It is about hugging them one by one.'

When any of Hana's people are hospitalized, Seung-Yu Kim always visits them in hospital. As the bank has 12,000 employees this is no mean feat. He also always attends the funerals of the parents of employees. 'Our people are like my family,' he explains. 'If they have some trouble, they call me up first.'

The e in communication

Whichever office I am in I always walk around and talk to people. I think it is great for taking the pulse of a firm and measuring morale. Nothing really replaces face-to-face contact, though of course there are many other means of communication available, from video conferencing, to handwritten notes.

'I'm in a technology-rich environment,' Patrick Swygert told me. 'I don't know how many emails I get a day, but however many I get, I send out probably an equal number. Email and my BlackBerry are pretty much how I communicate today. The telephone is becoming more the exception than the rule. On the campus [of Howard University], we have universal email, so you can send out a blast to all faculty, all students, all staff. It's so easy; but how many people actually read it is another matter.

'I took to heart a lesson that was given to me when I was an undergraduate. A professor told me, in the best of worlds you would speak to what you know with conviction, and you would speak to what you know with conviction in simple declaratory sentences. I've tried to do that my entire career. Sometimes with success, sometimes not.'

In the age of the Internet, many senior executives, including CEOs, offer their own weblog – a blog – as a source of communication. I began writing my own internal blog a couple of months into my time as CEO. I started it because I was aware that my office was often in darkness and my employees weren't too sure where I was or what I was up to. It's become a great way to stay in touch and I value the comments people leave me. The statistics about the number of abandoned blogs always motivate me to respond and post regularly. At the moment I have no plans to take my blog public but other CEOs have found this to be a persuasive marketing tool – Jonathan Schwartz, CEO and president of tech giant Sun Microsystems, David Neeleman, founder and CEO of JetBlue Airways, and Richard Edelman, of Edelman, the largest independent PR firm in the world, are all avid corporate bloggers.

What to say

Jacques Aigrain, CEO of Swiss Re, offered a number of thought-provoking observations about communication. 'It is quite a challenge to get some simple but motivating enough messages absorbed by the clerical staff, compared to the executive and management level,' he says. 'Especially if you're speaking about an esoteric risk business like ours, it can be horribly complicated in terms of the type of information you are dealing with to get the clerical staff to relate to what you are trying to do. Even in the communication with the professionals, across various specialities, it is not that simple to create a crisp, simple enough message that everybody can put their hands on.'

There are also the complexities of communication in a global business world. As Aigrain notes, most large companies involve a wide range of nationalities, who are often speaking English as their second language. 'In an ultra international organization where your home base accounts for a tiny part of your real business and where you have a huge mix of nationalities at every level, from the board of directors through every level, and thus the huge majority of the organization is not speaking English as their native language – including myself, that creates a second communication challenge.

'Obviously my use of English is not too bad but is not pure American or pure English, thus the choice of words, the expressions used, the mistakes made in using an idiomatic expression for the wrong purpose, all of that does accumulate in creating some confusion.'

Another important communication issue that CEOs point to is the need for effective education both internally and externally.

How do you communicate a message that is sufficiently consistent for all external purposes – for your investors, your stakeholders in terms of the local community, the press – as well as for internal ones? 'You cannot afford, in a public listed company, to have a significantly different communication internally and externally. You can have different nuances internally, but you cannot actually provide that much more data, as it becomes instantly disclosable. So you are considerably more limited now than you were ten or fifteen years ago,' Aigrain says.

'You need to have totally different types of communication internally than externally. So it becomes a question of layering – of having one fundamental storyline and then you peel off some more layers of the onions for the internal aspect, or you put some different emphasis or cast a different limelight for communication with the local community versus the investors.'

The communication coda

But communicating what? The best CEOs have an innate ability to identify what needs to be done today and what can wait. They know the key messages to communicate from day to day, from audience to audience. They prioritize constantly, aware that wars are lost by fighting on too many fronts. This requires a high degree of patience. 'Everyone feels we're moving like a bullet,' one CEO confided. 'But I feel like we're crawling.' Pace is relative.

I have been surprised by how I can be misunderstood – and for me it's not an English language problem, it is a question of understanding, emphasis and expression. I have modified how I speak, to make my vocabulary more simple and easy, in an attempt to get my message understood.

The reality is that each person reads material from their own perspective, taking their own meaning from what is written, and you need to try to predict that. That goes for both emails and spoken word.

I recently had a conversation in an office to do with how resources would be allocated. The feedback two days later was that there would be no resources for those billing insufficient fees. This was not my message at all, but Chinese whispers are powerfully loud.

Similarly, I sent an email about a change in personnel to the whole firm, and the message I got back from some quarters was that it was too harsh on this particular individual. It was hard to explain that the individual in question had actually checked and approved and helped write the announcement.

The reality is that you want to do the right thing and communicate and be clear and transparent but you have to spend so much time checking that the communication isn't possibly going to be misinterpreted, or misunderstood, by great sections of the organization that sometimes the timing is not as swift as you want it to be. And guess what? After all that, it still gets read the wrong way.

And as CEO, if someone complains to you, you can't say, 'Oh yeah, right, I know what you mean, XYZ is a pain.' You cannot jump on the bandwagon. And really you need to decide whether you want to be one of the gang or whether you want to be a leader of the firm – you cannot be both. I think that is a difficult transition for most CEOs.

The bottom line for myself and other CEOs is that I don't mind if people don't like me, that is human nature; but I want them to trust and respect me, and that takes time and is only possible with great communication, all the time.

My own take on communication is that it must follow a number of straightforward rules – eight, to be precise.

1. It must be simple

'Whatever the message is, it is important to make it simple. Complex messages are never understood. The only things that are going to be effective are things that are simple. Then people around you can understand and act on them,' says Carlos Ghosn. 'At Renault and Nissan, we have three- to four-year business plans with a maximum of three commitments that the company sets to achieve in order to keep the focus and to enable limited and concrete milestones and objectives.'

Complicated messages are harder to decipher. If you can say something simply, then do. This includes eradicating management speak and jargon. The legendary US investment guru Warren Buffett once opined that if he doesn't understand something, he assumes that someone is trying to fool him.

Plain speaking is not easy. Many organizations are steeped in a culture of management speak. Failure to communicate simply can be costly, however. In 1983, computer manufacturer Coleco wiped $35 million off its balance sheet in one quarter. The reason: customers found the manuals for a new product line unreadable and swamped the company with product returns. In 1984 the firm went bust.

Also, you can never assume that your audience is on the same wave-length. I went to a friend's 40th birthday dinner in the States. His daughter was asked to set the table. It was explained that the forks needed to be on the left and the knives on the right with their sharp sides pointed towards the plate. She got the forks right, but the knives were carefully placed at right angles to the plate. The girl had been helpful and had listened, but the final detail of communicating wasn't thought through. Imagine the room for misunderstanding in a global organization where there are, metaphorically at least, knives and forks everywhere.

2. It must be precise

Confusion is often the product of ambiguity. Don't say: 'I want the project tomorrow.' Specify what project, where you want it, and at what time. Much less margin for error. This way if you actually wanted the project on your desk in the morning, you won't be spend the day stressed out because the person delivering it thinks they have until midnight to email it to you.

3. Face-to-face is best – even now

In the information age we have a huge choice of communication media – email, telephone, video conferencing etc. However, evidence suggests that none are as effective as good old face-to-face interaction. About 80 per cent of human communication is non-verbal. Facial expressions, body language, eye contact – these are key conduits.

We read body language to pick up the atmosphere. We walk into a meeting and pick up the feel of what other people are thinking. We watch how Y reacts to what X is saying. You can't do that by video conference. Body language speaks volumes. Ignore it at your peril.

'I believe a word from my mouth, or from anyone, has a strong soul. If you talk directly instead of through email and as long as you have a strong will, you can convey your will. This is right, let's get things done,' says Takeshi Niinami, CEO of Lawson in Japan. In the early days as CEO, Takeshi estimates that he spent almost 70 per cent of his time talking and listening to people face to face.

Takeshi especially made use of team meetings. 'You can have direct communication with thirty or forty people, rather than using email. Actually I didn't use email at all – I just spoke on my own with the people. And I was always there at our training programmes at the Lawson University to talk to managers directly. Even now, for probably three months of the year, I'm not in the office at all. I'm out of town and don't come back to Tokyo.'

When I spoke to Monika Ribar she had travelled the previous week from her office in Europe to Latin America. The sole purpose of the visit was the retirement party for a long-standing employee and manager who had been with the company for over thirty years. 'The company sees that I am there and this is very, very motivating for people,' she says.

4. Make it personal

Flatter management structures mean that executives can no longer rely on hierarchical power to get things done. Instead, managers must increasingly rely on persuasion – and inspiration. This requires a more sophisticated style of communication directed at the individual and imbued with emotional context as well as content.

One survey of sixty executives found that the messages that get attention are those where the message is personalized, evokes an emotional response, comes from a trustworthy or respected sender, and is concise.

Great CEOs have long been aware of this. Jack Welch of GE habitually wrote handwritten notes which he sent to workers at all levels, from part-time staff to senior executives. Some even framed his notes, as a tangible proof of their leader's appreciation.

Seung-Yu Kim of Hana Financial Group told me about the amazing efforts he puts into establishing personal rapport with all the bank's employees. After Hana merged with several banks, Seung-Yu set out to memorize the names of many people as possible. He memorized almost one thousand.

'I had their photographs and their names, a CD in my car, and something on my desk, and even beside my bed. I tried to remember their names and their background, which province they came from, which school they graduated from. I tried to memorize them all. I also pop into branch offices whenever I can.'

5. Be yourself

Your communication style not only needs to be personal, it needs to be authentic too.

'There is absolutely no chance of winning if you are not yourself. If you're not yourself you stumble. Media training – to know their tricks? Absolutely. Basic communication experience? You learn on the job too. But just be yourself, because trying to be something else will create inconsistency between what you write and what you say, and how you say it,' says Swiss Re's Jacques Aigrain.

Aigrain admits to it taking some time for him to get this aspect of his communication strategy right. Authenticity can cause problems at first depending on your style; you have to see it through though, and not change because of the initial reactions.

'First there was a feeling that I was maybe too brutal from the perspective of the community at Swiss Re, that I was the so-called "bloody American banker type". Then phase two was, "He may be a shark, but he seems to say things that may make sense,"' says Aigrain. 'Finally, once they saw the results, came phase three, which is, "He has a big stick but he also means well and he cares, and he creates a dynamic and a momentum which we are ready to jump in." But, any variance in terms of the way I express myself or the tone that I used would have been interpreted inappropriately, and perceived as a fake.'

6. Watch the context

It is not just what is said that matters, but the setting in which it is said. Talking to the boss in the bar or over lunch in the restaurant is a world away from a one-to-one in the boss's office. There is often a power dynamic involved in the choice of location. Be aware of it.

I was struck by the importance of knowing your audience when I spoke with Carl Schramm of the Kaufmann Foundation, the leading foundation in the United States for promoting entrepreneurship. Carl is an author and actually says that he writes books for an audience of eight people – his board – and for the hundred people who work at the Foundation. Beyond that his work is picked up by many, many people, but he knows that the first two audiences are the ones which really matter. Every year Carl also writes a speech for the entire organization in which he maps out what the organization stands for and so forth. 'This is partially symbolic', Carl told me, 'because a lot of people here are treasury clerks and so forth. They know I'm out speaking to government ministers, politicians and CEOs. One of the implicit signals is, I stopped and wrote a speech for you because you're the people who count.'

7. Regularity breeds contentment

'I've learnt that people don't get the message until you hear it back from them. Once they're starting to repeat the message, then you know, okay, they're on the team,' says Sesame Workshop's Gary Knell.

Bruno Lafont, chairman and CEO of Lafarge told me that he reads only direct emails but maintains constant communication in other ways. 'I meet with my executive committee team for three hours every week, and meet with each of them individually once a month for one hour, and when needed. Together, every month, we review the advancement on the Group's few strategic and operational priorities. We have now quarterly business reviews and I attend many of them. I keep travelling a lot and try to meet informally as many local employees as possible, which ensures that I have a good understanding of what is going on in the business.'

CEOs who are good communicators know it is essential to maintain a frequent dialogue with their executive team. It is no use hauling an executive in to give them a roasting if you haven't spoken to them for the previous month. Regular dialogue should have removed the need for the dressing down. And remember that communication is a two-way activity. Key to this interaction is listening.

'I have a management team with five members and then there are regional CEOs all directly reporting to me,' says Panalpina's Monika Ribar. 'Now, what is very important is that we cascade down the communication. It starts with communicating clearly, simply and consistently. I think this is the most important thing. If you always tell the people the same story, if there is a change you need to announce it as a change and say I have made up my mind and it's not an X, it's a Y. This is so important.'

8. Be positive when you can

It is tempting to slide into negativity. There is a lot wrong in any organization – and that includes your own. No one you encounter is perfect – and nor are you. So, accentuate the positive and use positive reinforcement to back your strategies. This was brought home to me talking to Takeshi Niinami, CEO of Lawson.

One of his strategies was to make the company's local branches receptive to local needs rather than standardized by central dictate. 'We are everywhere in Japan and Japan has a very diverse culture and lifestyle. So we have to understand local customs and to match up with local customs. We can't decentralize customer needs,' he says.

When the first stores started matching with local needs, there was an expectation that the CEO would issue a reprimand. Standardization had been the policy. Instead, Takeshi Niinami praised the efforts of the stores in front of as many people as he could. 'These kinds of things easily fly all over Japan,' he says. 'Some products, local products or local rated products, were failures. But I didn't give them bad feedback. Basically, before I arrived people didn't want to challenge the status quo, they just listened to management. They never thought on their own. I just pushed people to think on their own.'

Key points

> The core in the CEO job description is communication.

> Communication must be constant and it must be simple, precise, face-to-face as much as possible, personal rather than standardized, and sensitive to context.

Resources

Bains, Gurnek et al., *Meaning, Inc.*, Profile, 2007.

Brown, John Seely, Groh, Katalina, Prusate, Laurence and Denning, Steve, *Storytelling in Organizations*, Butterworth Heinemann, 2004.

Denning, Stephen, *A Leader's Guide to Storytelling*, Pfeiffer Wiley, 2005.

Steel, Jon, *Perfect Pitch*, John Wiley, 2006.

Chapter **5**

The rise and rise of the global CEO

Increasingly, a CEO's work takes place in a global arena. What does this really mean? If you're CEO of a tractor parts manufacturer in Deerpark, Ohio, what does the world matter?

If I'm a 33- or 34-year old executive and I really want to do well, and my company has a global footprint, I've got to get out of Arlington, Virginia, at some point. I've got to be able to be flexible enough to do that, and then once landed in that otherwise alien environment, be open to its culture and language. You just can't stay put and be successful.

Patrick Swygert, President, Howard University

Global savvy

Globalization is a good thing.

Increasingly research supports this view. CEOs say that globalization is making business more complex but is having a positive impact on their organizations, according to a survey of 1,410 CEOs in 45 countries, published by PricewaterhouseCoopers. Internally, the factors that led to increased business complexity for CEOs to a large or very large extent included expanding their operations into new territories (65 per cent), engaging in mergers or acquisitions (65 per cent) and launching new products or services (58 per cent). Externally, complexity was driven to a large extent by international, national or industry-specific regulations, laws, standards and reporting requirements as well as by competitors' actions. Global growth is often centred on what Goldman Sachs has named the BRIC economies: Brazil, Russia, India and China.

Global expansion presents several challenges for CEOs to confront, including overregulation (64 per cent) and trade barriers/protectionism (63 per cent) as well as political instability (57 per cent) and social issues (56 per cent). But CEOs view globalization in a positive light, with 58 per cent saying it will have a positive impact on their firms in the next year and 63 per cent seeing a positive impact in the next three years.

Look around the highest echelons of the corporate world and, increasingly, you will see globalization at work. CEOs and senior executives are more of a diverse group than ever before, their backgrounds and careers impressively thick with global experiences. Times have changed. Back in the 1970s, an American executive was appointed to head the British coal industry. There was outrage at the very thought of such corporate carpetbagging. Would the same debate occur today? I very much doubt it. British Airways has an Irish CEO following on from an Australian; Vodafone is led by Arun Sarin, an Indian-American; the Americans Marjorie Scardino and Rose Marie Bravo run Pearson and Burberry respectively.

Today, global business is more than a political discussion point, marketing mantra or corporate aspiration; it is a burgeoning day-to-day reality. One need only scan trade statistics to understand why.

More than half the S&P 500 now report revenues by geography. For them, international markets account for 33 per cent of revenues – and their international business is growing nearly twice as fast as their US business (9.1 per cent annually versus 5.4 per cent between 1998 and 2003). Not only is trade becoming more global, the leading companies are as well.

The reality is that as the business world has globalized, so too has the executive job market and the job of CEO in particular. Measures of corporate or personal success are now gauged in global terms. Increasing market share in home markets is unlikely to suffice as a measure of success.

CEOs are measured against global performance. Asked about key measures of his long-term success, Michael Critelli, then CEO (and now chairman) of Pitney Bowes, cites globalizing his company as a central benchmark. 'We were a very insular US company which exported to certain markets and was predominately strong in English-speaking markets,' Critelli explains. 'I am very excited that we are in many markets today where English is not the only language spoken. I want us to be confident and comfortable dealing across the globe.'

Increasingly, there is a cadre of globally savvy CEOs who are, in Critelli's phrase, confident and comfortable wherever in the world they are doing business. Look at the names leading some of the world's biggest corporations. The world is their boardroom.

Coca-Cola is headed by E. Neville Isdell, a peripatetic Irishman who has worked for the company in Zambia, South Africa, Australia, the Philippines and Germany. (There's a story about Isdell I heard that when he was working in eastern Europe, he fitted out a van with a table and eight seats and then drove around making stops to visit with salespeople who climbed aboard the van to do their presentations.) The Alcoa CEO, Alain Belda, is a Brazilian citizen but was born in Morocco; Kellogg's CEO, Carlos Gutierrez, is Cuban; a Welshman runs L'Oréal; and the French Jean-Pierre Garnier heads GlaxoSmithKline.

Research by the Economist Intelligence Unit found that, of 250 companies in ten markets, the nationality of over 18 per cent of board members was different from that of the company they managed. This figure will certainly increase in the years to come.

The new breed

None of this should come as a surprise. There cannot be a significant company in the world which does not either compete globally or face global competition.

'The fact is that executive life has changed. Only 20 years ago, the capabilities required of successful executives were functionally oriented. Apart from occasional forays to overseas subsidiaries, executive life was monocultural. The role of senior executives was carefully – perhaps comfortably – delineated. Communication was local, personal, and managed to fit the executive's convenience. Markets were monolithic, and reassuringly stable,' say Laura Tyson, former dean of London Business School, and former GE executive Nigel Andrews who led a research project into the emerging training requirements of organizations based on more than one hundred face-to-face interviews with executives from global companies across a variety of industries and geographies.

'Globalization is not simply about the transfer of work to emerging economies. Globalization is an art – an art of human relations which, like other arts, is premised on insights gleaned from teaching and from experience, and honed by continual practice, day in and day out, in the executive suites of the world's corporations. Globalization is about the exercise of management and leadership, on a worldwide scale.'

As an exemplar of this new breed, consider Christopher Rodrigues, former CEO of Visa International, a business which recorded transactions of $4 trillion in 2006 thanks to its 1.2 billion cardholders.

Rodrigues is British but his résumé is global, including education at Cambridge University and Harvard Business School, experience with McKinsey & Company, and senior positions with American Express, Thomas Cook, and Bradford & Bingley, which he led through its demutualization.

Global CEOs such as Rodrigues offer a potent combination of skills and experiences. The box marked 'analysis' is ticked by Harvard and McKinsey. Then there is work with truly global organizations – American Express and Thomas Cook – as well as a change leadership role at Bradford & Bingley. The foundations to this are general management skills. Rodrigues worked in advertising and marketing – his first job was selling dog food from the back of a car – and then filled in the gaps in his knowledge of accounting at Harvard where he added a broad range of basic skills and some sense of their interaction. The final element to this is diplomacy. When Rodrigues got the Visa job, his background reading was Margaret MacMillan's *Paris 1919* which looks at the diplomatic machinations behind the creation of the League of Nations.

My view is that it is going to be very difficult to be a global CEO in the future unless you've experienced living in one or more regions. And companies who fail to give their individuals exposure to different cultures and a range of global experiences are going to lag behind.

Global CEO characteristics

But what are the characteristics and skills of these global CEOs? If you wished to create an identikit of the global CEO, it would run something like this.

First, they would possess experience in a number of global markets as well as experience in marketing, operations and finance. The résumé of

Chris Rodrigues is no longer a rarity in its geographical and functional reach. In their book *Why Should Anyone Be Led By You?*, Rob Goffee and Gareth Jones point to the powerful influence of early experience in the sales function.

Experience is essential but it must be interpreted and applied flexibly. Says Phil Hodgson, director of leadership programmes at Ashridge Business School in England: 'Older leaders need to work very hard not to let their decision making and their understanding of a situation be dominated by their past experience of success and failure. It is very hard to accept that what worked before may not, probably will not, work as well again. Equally, what failed last time does not necessarily define what will fail this time. The successful older leader stays successful by reinventing themselves so that they employ the learning without deploying the methods gleaned from yesteryear.'

The issue of age is also occupying the mind of Warren Bennis. Now in his late seventies, Bennis has grey hairs in abundance. As well as thinking about leadership, Bennis is a leader. In the Second World War, he was the youngest infantry officer in the US Army in Europe. 'It shaped me so much and pulled from me things I may never have experienced,' Bennis recalls. 'I was very shy and felt that I was a boring human being and then, in the course of being in the army, I felt that I was more interesting to myself. It was a coming of age – though I still didn't feel as though I was a leader.'

For Bennis the war was what he calls a 'crucible' – 'utterly transforming events or tests that individuals must pass through and make meaning from in order to learn, grow, and lead'. The trouble for youthful leaders is that crucibles are rare and cannot be artificially reproduced. You can't re-create Nelson Mandela's Robben Island.

Bennis's book *Geeks and Geezers* (co-authored with Robert Thomas) examines a selection of 'geeks', leaders between the ages of 21 and 35, and 'geezers', men and women between the ages of 70 and 93. For many of the older leaders, the war and the Depression were crucibles in which their values were formed.

'The geezers were brought up in survival mode,' Bennis explains. 'Often they grew up in some poverty with limited financial aspirations. They thought that earning $10,000 a year would have been enough. Compare that to the geeks, some of whom made a lot of money when they were young. They are operating out of a different context. If the geeks were broke they would be more concerned with making a living than making history.'

The message for would-be leaders is that leadership is founded on deeply felt experiences early in life. Youth may not be an obstacle to becoming a leader, but only if you have been through a crucible and emerged unscathed on the other side.

Culture clubs

A second element crucial to the global CEO relates to culture. The research at London Business School by Tyson and Andrews concluded that companies require executives with what they label global business capabilities: 'the power to think, decide and act efficiently and innovatively in an unpredictable global business environment'. Nowhere are these more vital than in the corner office of the CEO. Global CEOs need to be comfortable with people and comfortable with people from a range of cultures. The reality is that country-specific cultures are still important and need to be borne in mind by all business leaders.

There are many examples of business leaders who have tried to impose their way of doing things and have encountered culture-based resistance. It is still happening. Recently a US CEO was appointed to run a bank in Asia. He got there and told everyone that what they were doing was basically wrong, not the way it needed to be done. He lasted six months because, although he could run a US-based global bank, an Asia-based global bank offered an entirely different set of cultural challenges.

It is worth remembering that different ways of doing things offer different opportunities – both business and personal ones. The Indian electrical equipment company Anchor came up with a vegetarian toothpaste. Most varieties actually use a small amount of meat product in some way. For vegetarian Indians this was a definite non-starter. Anchor created a new niche in the market.

Being a global CEO requires a certain cultural sensitivity, as many CEOs have told me.

'Cultural awareness is important – being reasonably sensitive and aware of the differences and nuances between America and Europe, between the different countries in Europe and between Asia and the rest of the world,' says Jacques Aigrain. 'So being a global CEO is about cultural awareness – making people understand it is one single company, one pool of capital, one single duty to the shareholder and so not being particularly flexible with regards to local compromises.'

Not bowing to the demands of the local business at the expense of the global business is particularly important, emphasizes Aigrain. 'There are plenty of local rules and regulations, but absolutely no reason why the culture you create for the firm, and the way you want to do business, should be compromised by the perceived local circumstances. You want one standard, and from our perspective, you want to apply it in the same form everywhere. You don't want a local management which gets overly influenced by a local view, rather than the global interests of the firm.'

I realized early on when I came to Europe that my leadership approach would need to change. Americans and to some extent Asian countries generally enjoy a far more directive management approach. They expect the leader to lead. In Europe, I could not dictate and direct what I wanted to do (if I wanted anyone to actually do it). Instead I needed to consult and then discuss and listen to the thoughts of others. Even if I didn't use the suggestions given to me, the Europeans needed to be consulted. This did mean decisions took longer to make but in the long run it was worth it, and enabled me to gain the trust and loyalty of my European colleagues.

Staying power

A third element is sheer staying power. The skills required of global CEOs are demanding. So, too, is their schedule. Witness the travel plans of WPP CEO Sir Martin Sorrell: 'In the course of the year I go to one major region. So last year I did Latin America for two two-week trips. This year I'm doing Asia – alternate years I go to Asia, I'm going two or three times this year. Asia and Latin America as a proportion of our business is almost 25 per cent now so it's becoming increasingly important. I go to New York once or twice a month, usually for a week at a time. Europe I go to on usually one-, two- or three-day trips.'

Such schedules are not unusual. Indeed, if you run a global organization they are expected. Physically and mentally such levels of travel are demanding. (More of that later.)

The talent market

Tyson and Andrews' research at London Business School concluded that companies require executives with, 'the power to think, decide and act efficiently and innovatively in an unpredictable global business environment'. Nowhere are these more vital than in the corner office of the CEO.

The number of such accomplished – and energetic – global CEOs will undoubtedly continue to rise as the pace of globalization intensifies. Demand for global CEOs will grow. In India, for example, as companies expand they increasingly need business leaders who have broader international experience. Local managers can utilize plentiful Indian manpower, but it takes very different skills to launch products and brands in foreign markets.

This poses fundamental questions about how we prepare executives for leadership roles in global organizations. Indeed, some doubt whether ease with global business can be acquired. Gary Knell, CEO of Sesame Workshop, has worked extensively throughout the world. He worked in Asia at the time of the widespread economic collapse, and the handover of Hong Kong. 'It was a tumultuous time in business and economics. The baht was devalued overnight, the parent company I was working for had a lot of financial challenges and I was trying to manage the publishing piece of that company and we were cash-strapped,' Gary recalls. 'I was under fire. I had to make decisions about who would be on the payroll one day and who would not be and what bills we needed to pay on Friday or put off to the following week.

'First, it tested my executive decision making. Everything since that time almost pales in comparison with the pressure that I was under. Second was just being able to operate between cultures. I had a staff made up of virtually every ethnic group in the world from Singaporeans to New Zealanders to Brits to Americans to Thais and Chinese and Japanese. I loved that. I loved being around that kind of diversity.

'Executives either get how to work internationally or they don't. It's like it's genetic and it's really hard to teach someone how to work effectively on a global basis if they don't have it in their own blood. I think having a global perspective is something that really you have in your blood and it's not for everybody. There was an advertising campaign which asked: Is your company truly global or are you just all over the place? I always remember that because you can be all over the place or you can really have a global perspective. I try to surround myself with people who can understand a global perspective and go between cultures.'

Another CEO with formative global experience is Chip McClure of ArvinMeritor. 'Until I lived overseas, which was back in 1992 to 1995 in Germany, I don't think I really understood what it meant to be a global person. I had travelled extensively before that. I had spent a lot of time in Japan, I was responsible for many of our overseas joint ventures. But if I was honest about it, I would get on a plane, fly business class, go stay in a business hotel, be there Monday to Friday and then fly back home,' he told me. 'It wasn't until the first time, on a Sunday morning in the middle of winter that I had to call and try to communicate in German, to convince a plumber to come out and fix the heating system because the family was sitting there freezing, that I really realized what being a global person was.'

As Gary Knell and Chip McClure's comments suggest, the identikit global CEO I described is not the product of a two-year MBA programme, but the culmination of decades of development and experience in truly global settings. Such global *savoir faire* is not easily acquired. Given that fewer than 25 per cent of Americans have a passport, the number of potential global CEOs likely to emerge from the United States is more limited than you might think. 'There are very few American managers that really can think global,' says Monika Ribar of Panalpina. 'In Europe we are multicultural. Always have been.'

Nor is the global CEO necessarily provided by the world's business schools. At Harvard Business School, non-Americans are 33 per cent of the MBA intake. At the University of California's Anderson School the figure is 24 per cent. There is a long way to go if the undoubted future demand for global CEOs is ever to be met.

So, let's take a look at what needs to be done by companies in the global front line?

Take regular soundings

Companies have to create systems and networks which allow them to key into the major global trends. Lafarge has an international advisory board which helps alert the company to geopolitical and international trends. 'This is invaluable,' says Bruno Lafont, Lafarge's chairman and CEO. 'It gives us the opportunity to benefit from the experience of key international economic leaders. They contribute to the moulding of the Group's prospective international vision. We meet with them twice a year for a two-day session. One of the meetings is held in France and covers some of the biggest issues of the modern world such as environmental management, research, and cultural dialogue. The other meeting focuses on further understanding the development of a country or a region. The two last trips were dedicated to South Africa and China. There we listen to leaders on the political, economical and social aspects of the country. Industrial groups based in the country comment on the conditions in which they develop their business, overall giving Lafarge the benefit of their experience and a deeper understanding of geopolitical and economic trends.'

Acquire the talent

With deep and deepening pockets, it is now possible for some emergent companies to buy the talent they need. Lenovo's acquisition of IBM Consulting, for example, allowed Lenovo to absorb a cadre of globally trained managers into its organization. This is an option for companies with deep pockets, but assimilating people after an acquisition is notoriously difficult.

Invest in developing experience

'We have to develop people who can understand globally and locally,' says Takeshi Niinami, CEO of Lawson. Companies in both emerging and established economies need to invest in the middle ranks of executives to give them the necessary global experience to succeed in the future. Sending senior executives around the world is good, but it is not enough. Executives must be sent at a much earlier age to learn languages and understand different cultures. Immersion is more useful than accumulation of air miles.

Hire Indian and Asian talent

The onus is also on western companies to hire talent from Asia. They need to introduce high potential Asian executives into their systems early enough to inculcate them with their cultures and competences. They need to develop the management talent of the future. Most organizations don't do this. They look in local markets when they have to. This is a talent band aid.

Get on the road

I heard a story about a Korean CEO who was interested in an opportunity in Bangladesh. When he arrived in Bangladesh to meet the minster for telecommunications and to visit some potential sites he got in a car from the airport. The car made it a few yards before it was stoned by passers-by. There was a strike and no cars were allowed to be on the road. The CEO was undeterred. He eventually hired an ambulance for the day. Even during a strike, no one stones an ambulance.

As we have seen, the travel itineraries of global executives are daunting. But there is no substitute for being there, and being there long enough, to see and understand what's really happening. Too often, executives fly in, meet and greet local executives, and reboard the plane. They spend too much time travelling and not enough time looking, listening, talking and seeing local market realities with their own eyes. One retail chain opened a store in an Asian market in completely the wrong location. Why? When the team made a flying visit to locations, it was the rainy season and the roads were all washed out. Consequently, they made a costly mistake based on inaccurate local information. That isn't a mistake a truly global CEO would make.

'I change the people, rather than change their minds. It takes too long time to change their minds,' says Seung-Yu Kim of Hana Financial Group. 'So I now wait about six months or one year. If I notice they're not going to change their mind, I change the people. So that's why I try to find the right person. That's a key job for me: to find the right person. We don't care about nationality, so that's why we are now recruiting from China and we are seconding people to China to learn the Chinese language – about ten to fifteen people every year. It's very important to learn the language, and then start to try to understand their culture, and their mind. Now, we have about a hundred people who can speak Chinese and have five branch offices in China. There are also many Koreans living in southern California, especially the Los Angeles area; about 1 million Koreans. So now I am working with one of the investment banks to take over one of the Korean community banks over there. In that case, even though they're Korean and can speak Korean, their culture is different from pure Koreans. So we need to understand the Korean-American culture. We're sending our people to southern California to understand what they think about Korea, and what they think about America.'

Key points

> Globalization is a business reality for each and every CEO – or should be.

> Globally savvy CEOs have broad-ranging functional and international experience which they apply flexibly and appropriately. Their experience is not enshrined in stone, but open to new interpretations.

> In addition, they are sensitive to different cultures and the cultural nuances of different situations. They have the stamina necessary for global travel.

> The rise of the global CEO provides four challenges for organizations. (1) They must ensure that they acquire truly global executives. (2) They must invest in their development – global skills require global development. (3) They must, in particular, hire talent from the burgeoning Asian and Chinese economies. (4) They must encourage their people to get on the road.

Resources

Andrews, Nigel, 'Global business capabilities', *Business Strategy Review*, Summer 2004.

Bennis, Warren and Thomas, Robert, *Geeks and Geezers*, Harvard Businss School Press, 2002.

Crainer, Stuart, 'Christopher Rodrigues: Visa, vision and verification', *Business Strategy Review*, Summer 2006.

Goffee, Rob and Jones, Gareth, *Why Should Anyone Be Led By You?*, Harvard Business School Press, 2006.

PricewaterhouseCoopers, *9th Annual Global CEO Survey*, 2006.

Tyson, Laura and Andrews, Nigel, 'The upwardly global MBA', *Strategy+Business*, Fall 2004.

Chapter **6**

My board and I

It is the moment of truth: the first board meeting. How does it work? You barely know the people around the table and they expect you to have delivered sterling results instantly. How can you manage your board?

You shouldn't walk into a board meeting with a bunch of issues unresolved. I like to bring my board with me. I think it's very important that there's unanimity or pretty close consensus on the issue. That only comes, I think, from taking the time to hear people out and explain your position and having those private times to be able to make sure that everyone's on the same page.

Gary Knell, President and CEO, Sesame Workshop

Boardroom shifts

In corporations power has shifted. Boards are under intensifying pressure to meet ever more exacting corporate governance standards. One of the results of this is that one person feels the squeeze more than anyone else: the CEO. Boards are intent on passing the pressure down the chain. While the CEO once held power, increasingly it is now boards that call the shots by closely monitoring the CEO's performance and determining his or her successor.

One of the catalysts for this was undoubtedly the spate of corporate scandals at the turn of the new millennium. These have been examined from every angle. But, it is worth noting that when Jeffrey Sonnenfeld, a corporate governance expert based at the Yale School for Management, examined the boards at Enron, WorldCom and Tyco he found no broad patterns of incompetence or corruption. In fact, the boards of these companies often exhibited best governance practices in terms of structural and procedural issues – for example, the make-up of committees; attending meetings; board size and composition; and financial literacy. They also scored highly on accountability mechanisms such as codes of ethics and conflict of interest policies. In effect, they were 'good' boards, but they had limited knowledge of what was actually going on in the companies they purportedly led.

Waldemar Schmidt, chairman of Superfos and Thrane & Thrane, a board member of other companies, and formerly group chief executive of ISS, is one of Europe's most experienced board members. 'There has been quite a change in the way boards spend their time,' he reflects. 'In the past I would say that most boards spent 80–90 per cent of their time discussing day-to-day business and very little time on the future of the company. That is changing. I'm not saying it's 80 per cent strategy and 20 per cent control, but there is clearly a shift in how much time effective boards spend on looking ahead.'

Dick Beattie, chairman of law firm Simpson Thacher & Bartlett, believes the board should spend all its time on strategy and no time on the day-to-day mechanics of the organization.

Unhappy boards

The most reported-on manifestation of this shift in power is CEO turnover. The 2007 annual study of CEO succession undertaken by the consulting firm Booz Allen Hamilton concluded that 'boards of directors have become more responsive to shareholder and regulatory pressure, and are more proactive in ousting underperforming CEOs'. With high CEO turnover, boards spend more time dealing with succession issues. Indeed, the growing trend is for boards to spend more time on issues which would traditionally have been the domain of CEOs. 'Boards will become more deeply involved in creating value by helping management better identify threats and opportunities, by supporting management's efforts to effect major change, and by enhancing the quality of the management team,' concludes the Booz Allen research.

In 1995 just 2 per cent of CEOs left because of boardroom infighting, according to Booz Allen's 2007 CEO survey. By 2006 that figure had jumped to 11 per cent. In Europe, boards appear to have no compunction about getting involved when the CEO is failing to deliver the growth required, with boardroom power struggles leading to 22 per cent of CEO departures in 2006.

The list of CEOs who have recently departed after disagreements with their boards is long, and lengthening. They come from all industries and all types of organization. Back in 2000, Lloyd Ward reportedly resigned from Maytag in a disagreement with the board over the strategic outlook and direction of the company. Maytag went on to turn over two more CEOs over the next two years. Others with places in the boardroom-differences hall of misfortune include Iomega's Bruce Albertson, Buy.com's Gregory Hawkins, Equitel's Mary Walker (who resigned in July 2002 after joining the firm in May), Spectranetics' Joseph Largey, Swiss Life's Manfred Zobl, Motorola's Christopher Galvin, Office Depot's Bruce Nelson and Swiss Sarnafil's Peter Schildknecht.

Think back to Carly Fiorina's departure from the CEO's job at Hewlett-Packard (HP) in February 2005 after differences, widely reported in the media, with the company's board on how to execute HP's strategy. Or, consider Marsha Evans's resignation from the American Red Cross due to friction with the board of governors – Evans's predecessor, Dr Bernadine Healy, was also forced to resign partly because of disagreements with the board. The cast of corporate Caesars appears to be increasingly outnumbered by the growing population of boardroom Brutuses. 'Business has entered the era of the short-term chief executive,' notes Charles Lucier, senior vice president emeritus of Booz Allen Hamilton. 'The age of the ephemeral CEO is here.'

Faced with this shift in power, what can CEOs do?

Relax, it's only complexity

First, CEOs have to accept that they are, for better or worse, stuck in the middle. Shareholders, the board and employees all exert pressure on them – and there is also the increasingly demanding media to consider. They have to accept that this level of complexity comes with the job. There is no simple solution; no CEO-as-dictator option which can be speedily programmed into the organization's modus operandi.

Indeed, complexity is likely to increase. With private equity firms piling more money into markets and the rise (almost overnight) of consortium deals with multiple firms buying bigger companies, the boardroom dynamics are vastly different. CEOs need the ability and appetite to serve multiple owners. Leading a company backed by private equity is often far more complex than serving a public company. The sponsors, inevitably, behave like owners, and achieving consensus requires patience and ego management. This phenomenon, and the pressures it brings for CEOs, is likely to extend to Europe and Asia in the quest for bigger deals.

Only connect

Second, CEOs need to communicate more than ever before. The channel of communication between the CEO and the boardroom needs to be constantly open. In too many cases CEOs seek to communicate with their boards when problems are mounting. On the other side, boards are often tempted to spring issues on unsuspecting CEOs at board meetings. Gamesmanship helps neither side win the game.

'I spend a lot of time communicating to the board. One of the things I put down as a key objective is to make sure that I meet with every individual board member, at least once a year. I have one-on-one meetings with them, which means I fly wherever they are to either have lunch or dinner. I try to spend a couple of hours having face-to-face time with them,' says Chip McClure of ArvinMeritor. 'I would say the entire time I've been here the board has been very engaged. They really do take their oversight responsibility seriously. They don't micro-manage.'

Simpson Thacher & Bartlett chairman Dick Beattie tells me that what he expects from me as CEO is to 'provide strong leadership, set a "tone at the top" that is unquestionably fair, ethical, transparent and beyond reproach. The CEO must also have considerable energy and unrestrained curiosity. As chairman, I additionally expect the CEO to work closely with me in setting agendas, leading discussions and seeking help when needed.' And he hopes the CEO would 'look to a non-executive chairman, in addition to his or her being a confidant and personal adviser, to provide help with getting the most value from the board of directors and guiding the board in providing oversight on the strategic direction of the firm.'

The best CEOs spend time between the board meetings in touch with the board members, managing expectations, seeking advice, taking soundings.

'We are lucky enough at Swiss Re to have a formidable board, with a mix of experience in terms of industrial and business experience. In most instances, I am keen to have preliminary exchanges of ideas with one or other of the board members, and the chairman has always, right from the very start, encouraged me to do so,' says Jacques Aigrain.

'So, I have indeed a number of aspects where I test concept ideas with one of the other board members. I am spending more time with the chairman of the audit committee, that sounds relatively obvious, but I am also spending more specific time with some of the other board members for one area or the other where they have extremely strong experience that I can benefit from.'

Clear and regular communications can turn around problems. One Fortune 100 company's fortunes had declined over ten years. By the time its board looked for help it was in effect a turnaround. A new board with broader advisory skills took over, but within three years it became apparent that the new CEO, while effective at improving operations was not able to reposition the company's strategy. Eventually, another CEO was brought in. He created a weekly communication plan with the board to keep them abreast of the major strategic shifts and allowed an open forum in board meetings so that board members could witness first hand the executive team in action. In this case, open and consistent communication helped the nimbleness of the company's decision making.

Manage expectations and define the boundaries

'You have a group of former CEOs who think they know everything. The trick is to manage their expectations,' one CEO told me. Board members like to know what's going to happen next. In fact, 'no surprises' is the cardinal rule for managing boards. Board members don't want to see events unfold in the media; they require it first-hand.

'Rule number one, and it's probably the toughest rule to manage and to maintain, is no surprises,' says Patrick Swygert, president of Howard University. 'No one likes to be surprised. The board doesn't like to be surprised, and the CEO doesn't like to be surprised. It's much easier for the board to keep its end of the bargain because it's not operating the company. For the CEO it's much more difficult because every day can bring a surprise. Their challenge is to filter out unimportant things and elevate to the board those issues that really do require the board's attention. For me, that's the first rule of how to get along.

'The second rule is the contrary to something I was told which I violently disagree with – and, as I've gained more experience, I disagree with it even more. I was told that it's good to have a kind of creative tension between the board and the CEO. I violently disagree with that notion, not simply because of my own personal experience, but because the CEO in today's world has enough to deal with, and doesn't need to deal with something silly like creative tension. I've seen times where the CEO is so engaged in the care and feeding of the board that there comes a point when they have to tend to the business. You need people on a board who can give you the benefit of their experiences, and see issues through the prism of their experiences, and people who are there when you really need them at times of crisis, and hopefully those times are few and far between.'

Related to managing expectations is having clearly defined boundaries where responsibilities begin and end. Overlap is dangerous. The chairman runs the board and evaluates strategy, manages corporate governance and manages non-executives. The CEO runs the company and manages dialogue with shareholders. The best CEOs have a passionate and clear sense of the company's purpose and ambition.

Target and manage the chair

The relationship between the CEO and the chairman is key. 'I have a very close exchange with my chairman,' says Monika Ribar of Panalpina. 'I try to talk to him, certainly at least once a week or even twice a week, to inform him, to talk to him, to also get his feedback.'

Steve Tappin's work among CEOs found that about 25 per cent of CEOs see the chairman as a key part of their support network.

With boards becoming more independent and the chairman's role being split from the CEO, the CEO–chairman–board of directors relationship will be increasingly crucial to how a company performs.

Historically, the CEO and chairman roles were often combined in American corporations. Separation is now commonplace thanks to corporate governance guidelines requiring greater distance between the board and the CEO to encourage objectivity.

A study by the governance ratings firm GovernanceMetrics International (GMI) found that 95 per cent of the FTSE 350 firms rated by GMI split the roles of CEO and chairman. In France, where the combined CEO and chairman has traditionally been a powerful force, there is now movement in this direction, with companies such as Renault and Carrefour splitting the roles. In Germany, the roles of the chairman as head of the supervisory board and of the CEO as head of the management board are separated in law.

More companies are splitting the chairman and CEO positions between two people. A survey by Institutional Shareholder Services of 1,433 companies that make up the various Standard & Poor's indexes, including the S&P 500, found that 41 per cent had separate chairmen and CEO positions in 2006, up from 37 per cent in 2005.

Among the higher profile companies to split the jobs in 2006 was troubled Ford, where chairman Bill Ford Jr gave up the CEO post to newcomer Alan Mulally, who moved to the troubled car maker from Boeing.

It is also notable that some high profile CEOs have become chairmen of major corporations. This suggests that they see the roles as powerful rather than ambassadorial – examples include former Nokia CEO Jorma Ollia becoming chairman of Shell; and AstraZeneca recruiting Louis Schweitzer, the ex-Renault boss, as its chairman.

When it comes to healthy CEO–chairman relationships, best practice is rarely reported. Agreement between CEO and chairmen is not a great media story. There is a wide range of approaches. Some chairmen are hands-on whereas others have a light touch. There is no formula. Successful instances often involve founders moving from the CEO's job to become chairman. Consider Microsoft chairman and CEO Bill Gates handing over the CEO reins to long-time colleague Steve Ballmer in 2000; eBay company founder Pierre Omidyar becoming non-executive chairman with Meg Whitman as CEO; and Intel's Andy Grove becoming chairman with Craig Barrett as CEO.

There are other instances of a CEO and chairman working together to turn around an ailing company, or the chair acting as a supporter to help a new CEO make the transition into the role. But, it is a complicated relationship. The chairman can in effect fire the CEO. 'You can only have a *professional* relationship with your chairman,' one CEO told me.

Think team not board

In reality, the most effective boards are high performance teams. As with all effective teams, members have clearly defined roles, play to their strengths and complement each other. CEOs need to think of boards as part of their team rather than as a sometimes irritating supervisory body.

Looking at boards in this way offers a different and potentially important perspective. Jeffrey Sonnenfeld, senior associate dean for executive programmes at the Yale School of Management, and a corporate governance expert, has observed: 'We need to consider not only how we structure the work of a board but also how we manage the social system a board actually is. We'll be fighting the wrong war if we simply tighten procedural rules for boards and ignore their more pressing need – to be strong, high-functioning workgroups whose members trust and challenge one another and engage directly with senior managers on critical issues facing corporations.'

A similar perspective comes from boardroom expert Edward Lawler: 'A board is a group, perhaps in some cases a team. Boards need to be assessed by the same conditions and behaviours that lead groups to be effective.'

The future agenda

Boards are slowly starting to pay attention to the role that they were established for: as a sounding board for management. They are spending considerable time and energy thinking about the business, bringing their expertise to bear on issues of growth, and seeking to provide their companies with competitive advantage.

The future boardroom agenda is as complex as it is demanding. The hope must be that boards and CEOs establish their roles more clearly. With average chairman and CEO tenure now comparable, uncertainty demands clarity.

Takeshi Niinami, CEO of Lawson, told me of his experience in managing his board. 'First I explained my vision and the strategic directions, rather than the numbers. I created the total picture for Lawson. And I explained what I wanted to do for Lawson in five or six years' time and how that was different from the competition. That big picture was shown to the board and, at first, I got agreement from the board, in terms of the big picture, not the numbers. Only then did I talk about numbers. I believe, and I think I've got agreement from the board members, that company value is not created only by numbers, but by continuity, stability, reputation, and a lot of other factors. If they don't like my way, I cannot advance, anything. I talked to them one-on-one for many hours to let them understand my way.'

Another emerging issue is the role of independent directors. 'Increasingly, in the FTSE 100, they're starting to question the value of some of the non-executive directors,' says Steve Tappin of Heidrick & Struggles. 'What companies are now looking for is much more contribution from the non-execs. Can they contribute on strategy, or on the big deals? Can they be an ambassador to open doors? Have they got a reputation, and to what degree can that help with the City? And, they're looking for people who can contribute, and are passionate about the company.'

Testing ground

Having talked to various people about boards and thought about my relationship with my own board, I sat down with one more person to really understand how boards can, and sometimes do, work. That person was Jill Kanin-Lovers. Her insights were so valuable that I thought they would work better if I kept them together, as her coherent and persuasive take on boardroom life.

From 1998 to 2004, Jill was senior vice president of human resources and workplace management at Avon Products. Jill and her team supported Avon through a major transition, moving from a holding company to a globally integrated organization. Jill was a member of the company's executive committee, corporate compliance committee and the Avon Foundation Board.

Today, Jill is a member of the boards of directors for BearingPoint, Dot Foods, First Advantage, and Heidrick & Struggles. She is a member of the compensation committee at BearingPoint and chairs the committee for Dot Foods, First Advantage and Heidrick & Struggles. Jill also serves on the audit committee at Heidrick & Struggles and the nominating committee at First Advantage. Previously, Jill was on the board of Alpharma, a specialty pharmaceutical company, where she chaired the compensation committee. Jill has chaired four CEO succession/search committees. First, Jill talked about board/CEO relationship.

Board and the CEO relations

'The role that a good board plays will vary a lot depending on who the CEO is, and their experience. With a young, first-time CEO, or with a company which hasn't been public for all that long – a baby public company or a toddler if you will . . . The support each CEO needs is different.

'The experience of sitting on a board is very different, depending upon the experience base of the CEO, what they expect from you, and what you feel you can contribute. Certainly in every situation you're there to represent the shareholders – that is your number one objective – but part of representing the shareholder is to make sure that the CEO and the management team are successful in what they're setting out to do.

'The press can give a very negative picture of board–CEO relations. Although the story at somewhere like Hewlett-Packard was extraordinary. There you have a situation where the board not only did not support the CEO, but there were some members who were obviously looking to undermine the CEO. I've never been in a situation like that though I have been in situations where the board was not satisfied with the performance of the CEO. The idea of the board undermining the CEO is just staggering to me.

'I've heard it said that the board provides the cheapest advice the CEO will ever get. I've been a consultant for a large part of my career and, as a board member, the company and CEO have free access to me. That's why I think who you put on your board also is very important. It is not uncommon when someone becomes the new CEO, and they take a look at the board, for them to say, "Hey, I could use maybe some counsel in this area and I don't see it reflected on this board", or, "You know, maybe there are folks on this board who I don't think are giving me fresh thinking." Not only do we provide oversight, but we're in essence a tool, a resource to the CEO, and they want to make sure they've got the right composition to reflect that.'

Diversity of thought

'You certainly want diversity of thought but you don't want people on the board who can't collaborate. You want different perspectives, and fresh thinking, but you need people who can also work with other people. If you wind up with people who are combative it's not really helpful. I think it is important to have people who can be independent but be collaborative at the same time. And you certainly don't need people to be on your board who think they should be running the company, either.'

Day-to-day versus strategic

'If a company is in trouble a good board will get more actively involved. But when a company is not in trouble it's really important that you draw the right line between operation and strategy, or operations and what the board should be doing. Management and the board need to work together, but they don't do the same thing. Sometimes I think it is hard for some board members to draw that line as to what's operational and what's more strategic. I think we should spend as little time as possible on day-to-day issues. Because that's really management's role. Now, if we don't think management is doing their job, you can talk to the CEO and counsel them that they may need to put a different leader or leaders in place.'

Trusted adviser

'I have found the biggest mistake many CEOs make is that they don't move quickly enough on the people they have surrounding them. And that's where the board may be able to say, "Listen, you know, it's time to take a really hard look at this – I know you like Joe, and you were invited to his kids' weddings, but this person is not doing the company or the shareholders any good." I just had this come up on one of my other boards – the management team had somebody who they liked, but they knew they weren't doing the job as well as they could, and they were thinking of bringing somebody else in, and they were going to organize around the individual. The board can be a great sounding board for saying, "Wait a second, do stop and think if you're doing something that in the long run you're going to be sorry about."

'When a new CEO starts there is definitely a honeymoon period but I suspect that is going to vary by how the business is doing. If the business is terrible, then the board probably won't be as patient. Which brings me to an important point, that is, selection. You want to get a CEO in there from the start who can get in pretty quickly, and who's a quick study. And that comes down to the whole concept of how the board selects a CEO. You don't want someone who is going to sit back and do two years of planning.'

Succession

'For a board to fulfil its fiduciary responsibility it must have a solid view of talent in the organization and feel confident that the company has the right leadership in place now and is constantly planning for the future. I think it's the most important job the board does. It's making sure that you've got the right person in place as CEO and staying with that person, and giving them all the counsel you can, but knowing that behind them there is a successor, ready to step in when necessary.

'It is very important for ambitious leaders to become known by the board, and while it's nice to meet staff members at a board cocktail party, the key players in the firm should actually do presentations to the board and have a real dialogue. Companies do that in different ways, for example asking the business unit heads to present their budget strategies to the board. Or, on one of my boards they actually have an entire day that's spent just on strategy, and they bring in different business heads to talk about their individual areas. Another board I sit on is just starting a new process where, at each board meeting, one business unit will be 'featured'. This deep dive on to a particular business unit means we, as board members, not only get comfortable with the various business centres, but we also learn the balance between the different businesses and the personalities behind them.'

How a board expects to be treated

'The basic rule in terms of treatment of the board by the CEO is that I don't want to read about it in the *Wall Street Journal*. Some stuff is operational and they should be running their business, but I can't see any advantage to keeping a deep dark secret on something that's a problem. Because it's going to come out eventually, and then you're going to get questioned as to why on earth you didn't say something sooner. The board is the cheapest counsel you'll ever get, so if you're dealing with an issue there should hopefully be somebody on your board who can help, and who you can reach out to.

'You have to have a mature relationship, and anybody who's on a board has to be willing to say, "You know what? That really didn't please me." The number one way to communicate is the direct way. If you have a separation of a CEO and chairman, then you also have another avenue for communicating, and the chairman can be the message carrier. We do an annual review of CEO performance, on all my boards. So the CEOs will be getting specific feedback on their behaviour. So if it hasn't been brought up directly, which is my preferred approach, then it should certainly appear in that performance review.'

Keeping up with communications

'To be a board member, I think you have to be an avid reader. You get lots of material from the company, and I always want to have more, rather than less, and then weed it out myself. I can't read every single analyst's report, thank you very much, but I like getting an overview on them. And I spend a lot of time on the phone. I mean, this past Friday I had three boards contacting me on the same day, on different issues, so I was on the phone for most of the afternoon, on things that were important to those different boards.

'You're independent, but you also have a real interest in the company, and you want to see it work. Everybody wants to be involved with something that is successful. And it's great when you see you've picked the right candidate as CEO and you look at all the great things they're doing, and what they're making happen. There is a great feeling of pride when you see the new candidate doing very well.'

Audit and compensation committees

'When I was told I was going to be on the audit committee of Heidrick & Struggles, I groaned, because you hear of all these endless meetings and pressure. But I now believe it is the best place to learn about the operations of the company and it has been invaluable to me in getting up to speed on Heidrick & Struggles' business. I also think it has helped me to be a more effective board member on my other boards.

'In audit meetings there is nowhere to hide in terms of how the organization is running, and I think if a CEO is able to attend these committees it constitutes a great learning tool.

'In terms of the compensation committee, which I also sit on, it is important for the CEO to be involved as he needs to be seen to lead the payment programme. There is a difference between the two: the audit is overseeing, the compensation committee is driving through projects that support the strategy.'

Key points

> The world's boards exercise more power than ever before. CEOs are increasingly feeling the pressure – especially when the jobs of chairman and CEO are separated.

> To a large extent, CEOs have to accept that the relationship between the CEO and the board is always likely to be complex and somewhat ambiguous.

> Successfully managing the relationship with the boardroom requires that CEOs first of all communicate regularly with all directors. They must manage the expectations of the board and make it clear where the boundaries of responsibilities lie.

> The key relationship is between the chairman and the CEO. This must be actively managed by the CEO wherever possible.

> The best boards operate as teams. The CEO needs to be the quarter back.

Resources

Charan, Ram, *Boards That Deliver*, Pfeiffer Wiley, 2005.

Conger, Jay A., Lawler, Edward E. and Finegold, David, *Corporate Boards: New Strategies for Adding Value at the Top*, Jossey-Bass, 2001.

GovernanceMetrics International, 'New global governance rating', 6 March 2005.

Institutional Shareholder Services, *Global Investor Study*, ISS, 2006.

Kakabadse, Andrew and Kakabadse, Nada, *Leading the Board*, Palgrave, 2008.

Leblanc, Richard and Gillies, James, *Inside the Boardroom*, Wiley, 2005.

Lucier, Chuck, Wheeler, Steven and Habbel, Rolf, 'CEO Succession 2006: the era of the inclusive leader', Booz Allen's annual CEO succession study, *Strategy+Business*, Summer 2007.

Peters, Georgina, 'Boards' eye view', *Business Strategy Review*, Summer 2006.

Chapter **7**

Me myself I

You're under pressure from all sides – investors, your board, not to mention your people, unions, competitors . . . and more. How can you keep your sanity and live happily when you could – should? – be working and travelling 24/7?

We demand a lot from our top people. More now than perhaps at any other point in the last century. Forget about 9 to 5, or 7 to 7, or 6 till 10. The cellphone, Internet and BlackBerry changed all that. Now we can work 24 hours a day, across every region in the world. Ever spent an afternoon at the in-laws' quietly closing a deal? I have. Ever gone on vacation and thought, just a little peek at my email won't hurt?

a CEO

There's always more to give

As a CEO it doesn't take long to realize that it is a very different job from any other position. For me, it seemed straightforward. It was 'just' a promotion. My employer didn't change. I grew up in Heidrick & Struggles and have friends and colleagues whom I have worked and played with for years. Suddenly, though, when I became CEO, people stood outside my office talking, but wouldn't come in.

That wasn't the only change. My days were longer and busier than ever. Although I was based in London at the time, I needed to be visible to all our offices across the world. I travelled constantly. The impression the leader portrays tells people how the company is doing; I needed to be up, positive and engaged, all the time. And still do.

Inevitably, it takes a toll on home life. I'm on the phone one minute talking to my CFO, the next I'm arriving home to be greeted by my eight-year-old daughter and the first thing she asks, 'Dad, do you know where my Nintendo DS is?' I routinely eat dinner standing up in the kitchen, because everyone else has eaten already and I only have an hour and a half before the next conference call. When my son's tooth fell out, the 'tooth fairy' only had euros and dollars in his pocket; not much good for a little boy expecting pound coins under his pillow.

One night I read my four-year-old son a bedtime story and he asked, 'Daddy, are you travelling this week?'

'Only to Germany for one day,' I replied. 'I'll be back in time to read you a story.'

'Dad, where is Germany? Is that near the grocery store?'

Actually, I have found that I don't talk about work at home – you almost don't want to relive it all again. It's a challenge, because you're dealing with work issues all day, from early morning, until you get home at 8 pm or later. And you want to switch off. You don't want to relive anything; you want to sit and unwind and relax in your comfort zone. It was tougher when my children were younger, because I'd walk in the door and my wife would hand me a baby – 'Can I just get five minutes to take off my suit first?' I'd ask!

Like many CEOs, I inhabit two separate worlds, with everyone demanding my time and attention. Sometimes I worry whether I have enough to give. One day I read a book called *The Giving Tree* by Shel Silverstein to my youngest son. It is a story about a tree and a little boy.

Every day the boy comes to swing on the tree's branches, to eat its apples and sleep in its shade. The boy loves the tree. And the tree loves the boy. But as the years pass the boy finds other things to do and the tree is often alone.

After much time has passed, the boy comes to the tree and asks for money. The tree suggests he picks its apples and sells them in the city. This makes the boy happy; he picks all the apples and goes away. And he stays away for a long time.

One day the boy comes back – he wants to build himself a house. The tree suggests he cuts off its branches. This makes the boy happy; he cuts off all of the tree's branches and goes away to build his house.

He stays away for a long time and is old when he returns. He is unhappy and fed up with life and wants a boat so that he can sail far away. The tree tells him to saw its trunk in two and make a boat. This makes the boy happy; he hollows the tree's trunk into a boat and sails away.

The tree (now a tree stump) is alone. After many years, the boy comes back; he is now very old and sad. And the tree is sad too, because he feels he has nothing left to give the boy.

The boy tells the tree that he is just so very tired and needs to sit down. The tree suggests that the boy sits on his stump and rests. And the boy does, and the tree is happy; it was wrong when it thought it had no more to give the boy.

Being a CEO can feel like being a giving tree. At work, and at home, people need you to give more. I am learning to embrace and understand this; and to view it as a privilege rather than a hardship.

Hard at work

I am not alone. There may be giving trees, but there are also unforgiving trees. I was talking with Richard Baker, CEO of Alliance Boots, and he told me a story about how he broke his shoulder when he fell out of a tree because he was just trying to be a good dad. His daughter wanted to climb a tree but he was tired from jet lag and working away all week, so he wasn't really concentrating as he climbed. He missed his step and fell to the ground. Tired CEOs and trees don't mix.

All the CEOs I talked to, and have talked to over the years, reveal much the same trouble with balancing hectic schedules and family life. I asked Monika Ribar of Panalpina how she spends her time. Her reply was typical. 'I constantly exchange information with my people. I'm looking at putting the right people in the right places. I meet with people, some of whom I want to hire. Then, of course, when I travel, companies give me presentations and we have discussions. Certainly the biggest part of my time, in the office or also when I'm travelling, is spent talking to people. And then there is preparing for meetings, especially executive board meetings or actual board meetings. Finally, there are all the presentations I give. At the moment, everybody wants me for a speech – there are not that many women CEOs.'

One of the striking features of globalization is that it is creating a 24/7/365 (24 hours a day, 7 days a week, 365 days a year) business culture. Depending on your point of view this is either a good thing or a bad thing. But it is also making the job of the CEO a 24/7/365 watch.

Overwork is not good for CEO health. Nor is it good for business. In the United States, a National Sleep Foundation study found that people who work more than 60 hours a week make almost 10 per cent more mistakes on the job than people who work less.

For many CEOs, burning the corporate candle at both ends and in the middle is a fact of life. A report at the 1999 Davos World Economic Forum put it succinctly: 'CEOs are increasingly suffering from stress, sleep deprivation, heart disease, loneliness, failed marriages, and depression, among other problems. And those woes are taking a toll on the bottom-line. CEOs must avoid workaholism. No matter how much they enjoy their jobs, they must avoid overworking when it renders their home life so unpleasant that the office becomes happier than the home.'

It's hard to argue with such sentiments, but the reality is often stark. One survey found that nearly one in two CEOs in Canada placed their firms ahead of their families in importance. The number who would not cut short a business meeting to celebrate their wedding anniversary was also nearly one in two.

There's one person whose emails I always read – my wife's. I remember one particular email, which I received on my BlackBerry just as I touched down in Hong Kong for a three-week trip to Asia. The email was empty but the subject line read, 'You forgot to change the light bulbs'. It was the one thing she had asked me to do before I left.

I was thinking my next book would be called 'Husband or Wife of a CEO'. During the research for this book, the incredible patience of the CEO spouse has come up again and again. CEOs nearly always mention their home life and the insight and support they couldn't do without.

'I see two types of CEOs: some of them are obsessed by their businesses, and it is really a lot of their life; and there's another group who see it as a big part of their life, but their family is important to them, and they need a life for themselves. And, a lot of those CEOs are supported by long-term family relationships, and families, and they seem to be more focused on looking after their watch, and then building a legacy,' says Steve Tappin. 'The relentless CEOs keep going until the company is number one, and is perceived as number one. For the others see, if they've taken the company forward and they've looked after all the stakeholders, the company's been successful. These are the more balanced CEOs.'

Balancing the week

Definitely in the balanced CEO category is Chip McClure of ArvinMeritor. I asked him about his schedule. 'I tend to get in early. I think the only person that gets in before me in the morning is my CFO. I'm usually in by 6.30; he's in by 6.00 so he's got the coffee made, which is nice,' he told me. 'There is no average week. If I look at my calendar for a full year, there's obviously certain things which are locked in – starting with board meetings, committee meetings, various shareholder meetings, analyst meetings, earnings calls, that type of thing. So within each week there may be those kind of things interspersed.

'If I look at next week, on Monday, I'm meeting with one of our heavy truck customers; on Tuesday and Wednesday, I'm going to be in Washington, DC. One of the things I try to do is spend time in Washington not only as a representative for the company, but also to represent the automotive industry. So, I've got a number of [Capitol] Hill visits with senators, and congress people. Then on Thursday I'm visiting with a company that's totally outside of our industry, just to do some benchmarking on technology. The company I'm meeting with has done a tremendous job reinventing itself by developing innovative technology. Then the following week I'll be visiting some of our global facilities. Two weeks ago I was in Mexico and visited six or seven of our plants. Obviously, I spent the majority of my time with our people, but at a few of the facilities I also took the time to meet with some of the local elected officials.'

Chip is famed for his ability to ensure that meetings run on time. 'The only thing you can't recapture is time,' he says. He has three strategically placed clocks in his office. He said, 'These clocks are in place because I don't normally like meetings to last more than an hour. I understand that sometimes a meeting might have to go a little longer because of the content, but when we hit 45 minutes and haven't gotten through all of the items, I'll say, "Listen, we've got 15 minutes left, what do we need to get resolved? Let's get it resolved, and let's move on. Because there's only 24 hours in a day." '

Present and incorrect

The problem with their unrelenting schedules is that CEOs set the pattern for everyone in the organization. Executives quickly learn to imitate the style of the person at the top. If that person is a workaholic – as virtually all CEOs are – its hardly surprising that the cult of presenteeism contin-ues. American CEOs tend to be among the worst offenders. 'Americans have more money because they have less leisure,' MIT's Lester Thurow has simply noted.

This is not just an American thing. A five-year tracking study carried out by Les Worrall and Cary Cooper for the UK's Institute of Management and the University of Manchester Institute of Science and Technology found that the work and home life balance was still a pipe dream. Over 80 per cent of executives worked over 40 hours a week and one in ten worked over 60 hours. A resounding – though depressing – 86 per cent said that the long hours had an effect on their relationship with their children and 71 per cent said that it damaged their health.

'We want to have it all. More money – and more time. More success – a more satisfying family life. More creature comforts – and more sanity. We can work hard, we can find love and have a family, and we can enjoy the fruits of our success,' concludes a survey by *Fast Company* magazine and Roper Starch Worldwide. It is a sobering thought, that several disasters over the past twenty years involved employee sleep deprivation, including Chernobyl, the *Challenger* explosion and the Exxon Valdez oil spill.

Many of today's CEOs could learn a lesson from another famous busi-ness leader of the past: John D. Rockefeller, president of Standard Oil. During his lifetime Rockefeller came in for much criticism, as well as some odd mythologizing. A persistent story was of his phenomenal capacity for hard work and long hours, a trait which Rockefeller strenuously denied.

'People persist in thinking that I was a tremendous worker, always at it, early and late, winter and summer,' said Rockefeller. 'The real truth is that I was what would now be called a "slacker" after I reached my middle thirties. . . .I never, from the time I first entered an office, let business engross all my time and attention.'

Rockefeller lived to the ripe old age of 97.

On the road

Energy, though, is undoubtedly a prerequisite for the job. CEOs also expect it of the people they work with. 'One of the things I look for most in people is energy levels,' Robert Devereux, former CEO of Virgin Group, observed. 'I won't employ people who don't have high energy levels, because they won't last. Because people with energy, they're self-motivated, they get going, they get things done.'

Yes, you need energy to be a CEO, and the more you have the better. Energy levels are most obviously tested by the vast amounts of travel which come as part of the job. 'I travel a great deal,' one CEO told me. 'My home office is in a suburb of Washington, DC, but I spent a great deal of my time on the road – in excess of 50 per cent. So I am in the office less than half the time.'

That's pretty typical. The reality as a twenty-first century CEO is that you are on the road most of the week. You do overnight flights because you're commuting, and when you get to the weekend, you're tired, and perhaps not as patient as you should be.

I recently had breakfast with a CEO in Asia. I said, 'So you flew in last night – how was your dinner?' He said, 'I had the standard dinner, from the mini bar – scotch and some peanuts.' I laughed, because I know how accurate that is.

Personally, I don't mind the flying because it is a great time to catch up on reading articles, books, client information and magazines. Every CEO I know reads a lot, and all the time, and they all say that they need more time to read – but who doesn't?

Having said that, the jet lag can be really tough. Like anyone else, I sometimes struggle in the afternoon: it's not like you become superhuman when you become CEO; it still hits you. I don't sleep well – but I think most leaders would say the same, and most people I know in leadership keep a notebook by their bed to remember all those thoughts that come to them as they lie awake in the middle of the night. And most would also agree that when they write that one thought down and switch off the lamp, they think of another five they want to write down.

Roads well travelled

It is worth remembering that today's travelling CEOs follow in a long tradition. From the earliest times, trade has relied on the willingness of individuals to suffer personal privation and hardship to transport themselves and their merchandise to their customers. One of the most celebrated western business travellers was Marco Polo, who chronicled his travels in China, accompanying his father and uncle on a protracted business trip in the thirteenth century. But long before Marco Polo wrote of his adventures, merchants were conducting business in strange and exotic lands.

Business travel is as old as business itself. Records show that as far back as the seventh century AD, the Silk Road – not one road, in fact, but many – was peopled by itinerant businesspeople plying their trade in everything from silk and spices to Buddhist scriptures. The city of Chang'an in China, the starting point of the great silk route, which stood where Xian is today, grew fat on the exploits of these early mercantile travellers. The 754 AD census of the city indicates more than five thousand foreigners based in the city, from as far afield as India, Japan and Malaysia. The route was a conduit for rare plants, medicines and textiles which were traded in the city's bazaars. In those days, the representatives of the emperor took their pick of the goods before trade could commence. The emperors have gone, but the need to understand local traditions and comply with the relevant authorities remains integral to the business traveller's licence to operate. Today, navigating cultural nuances and national laws still requires a deep knowledge.

Why travel?

The reality is that extensive travelling is a prerequisite for CEOs if they are to help their organizations maintain their competitive edge. 'The winners are going to be those people who can connect and collaborate, at lightning speed, across markets, geographies, time zones, demographics, and more,' says Kevin Roberts, worldwide CEO of global communications organization Saatchi & Saatchi. During one twelve-month period Roberts spent 175 nights in hotels on business travel.

Business relationships are based on communication and, as we've seen, communication is the cornerstone of the CEO's job. The question is why all the new communication media have failed to make a dent in travel schedules? The answer seems to lie with a simple statistic. More than 80 per cent of human communication is non-verbal (some studies put it as high as 93 per cent). In other words, email, telephone, video conferencing, and all the other communications marvels do not have the bandwidth to carry more than 20 per cent of the face-to-face experience.

Facial expressions, body language, eye contact – these are key conduits. Without them you can't get past first base. It's tough to bond over the Internet. So, unless your client is in the next office, to do business you have to travel. How else can you meet customers, colleagues and competitors? 'A CEO from Switzerland told me once that he has a personal key performance indicator that he wants to meet twice as many customers as investors and I think that's a very good target,' says Monika Ribar of Panalpina.

The downsides of constant travel are well documented, and justifiably so. Less emphasized are the plus sides. As a well-travelled CEO you get to meet a huge number of people and develop relationships which are important to them as businesspeople and as human beings. Travel allows people to connect. It can be a richly rewarding personal experience. Travel not only broadens the expense account. Business trips offer new and exciting vistas.

Surveys consistently show that young people entering the workforce regard travel as a perk. A survey of 350 Oxford University students in their final year of study, for example, sought to understand what motivates young people to join established firms. The survey found that foreign travel was among the factors most valued by the students, surpassed only by achieving the right balance between work and leisure – and pay.

Loyal supporters

With huge demands on your limited time and a punishing travel schedule, the CEO – any CEO – needs support.

Many companies now have a chief operating officer (COO) who manages internally, while the CEO devotes more attention to what's going on outside. It is not a new idea. There are precedents. Examples of famous business double acts abound. Think of David Hewlett and Bill Packard, James Hanson and Gordon White, Microsoft founders Bill Gates and Paul Allen, Body Shop's Gordon and Anita Roddick. Richard Branson relies on his sidekick of many years, Will Whitehorn. More recently, David Filo and Jerry Yang, the founders of Yahoo!, styled themselves chief Yahoos.

Stephen Miles, a partner in Leadership Consulting at Heidrick & Struggles, has done a lot of work on the role of the COO. He sounds a note of caution about the COO/CEO relationship in his book (co-authored with Nathan Bennett) *Riding Shotgun*. He notes: 'The key ingredient for COO effectiveness is often whether the CEO is ready to share power. Unfortunately some COOs do not realize the CEO is not ready until they are in the position and friction begins to appear in the relationship.'

But most CEOs today, at least in theory, seem to understand that solo leadership in the corporate world is ultimately inefficient and ineffective. No one individual, no matter how gifted, can be right all the time; no one individual, particularly in a large organization, has the relevant information to make every important decision. Over time, resources become misallocated, opportunities are missed, innovation becomes stifled. Over-control saps initiative and bureaucratic behaviour ensues.

'If you are working for a large firm, there are a number of tensions that managers deal with. Paying attention to clients and paying attention to operations, paying attention to the outside or inside of the organization, paying attention to the future, or to the present. You are focused on a strategy or on tactics. You are focused on control, or innovation; on numbers or on people; on maintenance, or change,' says José Luis Álvarez, associate dean at the Instituto de Empresa Business School in Spain. 'There are so many dilemmas that no manager could cope with all of them, at least not simultaneously. The more complex the organization, the more that power sharing makes sense.'

Whether you like it or not, a CEO has to rely on others – their secretary; their spouse; their colleagues; their team; their friends; their BlackBerry and many more. If you fly solo you go round in circles.

Role models

What is amazing talking to CEOs is often how much help and support they derive from early role models. Chip McClure continues to cite the advice of one of his company's bankers, Gene Miller. 'Gene said one of the things he learnt early on was the responsibility which lay in his title, CEO. He said the C is for customers, the E is for employees and the O is for owners, that's who I am responsible to. I have always carried that as my mantra. I've changed it a little bit and refer to it now as C^2EO because the second C to me is also the community. So I define my title as C^2EO, which is Customer, Community, Employees and Owners.'

For the past thirty years, Seung-Yu Kim of Hana Financial Group has had an epigram from Alfred P. Sloan mounted in a frame in his office. 'The circumstances of the ever-changing market and ever-changing product are capable of breaking any business organization if that organization is unprepared for change.' Sloan was the industry-shaping CEO of General Motors during its early development. The same wise words are mounted at the entrance of MIT's Sloan Management School to remind its students of the importance of markets, customers and innovation.

'Only companies which foresee market trends and proactively confront them may lead the market, and the financial industry is not an exception. As Hana Bank rose to become one of Korea's big four financial groups, at every single crossroads our people's efforts and mindsets effectively corresponded to changes in the market and our customers' expectations. During my career, I have never forgotten Mr Sloan's lesson and will cherish it for the rest of my service,' says Seung-Yu Kim.

Apart from Sloan, Seung-Yu Kim cites another role model: Jung-Ho Kim, the head of the branch where he started his career in the finance industry.

'He was a leader with great discipline,' Seung-Yu Kim recalls. A newcomer who could not calculate on an abacus had to come to the office by 7 am and practise for an hour before our daily business. And after business hours, we had to attend classes held by junior managers. He always sat at the back and did not leave until the end of the class. Being the first to arrive and the last to leave, he even volunteered for chores such as separating old currencies. Sometimes his professionalism made some of us uncomfortable, but none of us doubted his leadership.

'I still remember him saying, "The life of a banker lies in his honesty", as I heard it so many times. Whenever we received incentive payments for our performance, he handed it to each of us and reminded us, "You earned this with your hardships. Do not waste it. Save it." After a year of working under his guidance, he was transferred to another branch, but my memories of him stay with me.'

My role models are in the more distant past: the wisdom of Gandhi and Abraham Lincoln and the speeches of Theodore Roosevelt. There is one speech of Teddy Roosevelt's that I find particularly valuable. Speaking in Paris in 1910, Roosevelt said: 'It is not the critic who counts: not the man who points out how the strong man stumbles or where the doer of deeds could have done better. The credit belongs to the man who is actually in the arena, whose face is marred by dust and sweat and blood, who strives valiantly, who errs and comes up short again and again, because there is no effort without error or shortcoming, but who knows the great enthusiasms, the great devotions, who spends himself for a worthy cause; who, at the best, knows, in the end, the triumph of high achievement, and who, at the worst, if he fails, at least he fails while daring greatly, so that his place shall never be with those cold and timid souls who knew neither victory nor defeat.' That's pretty inspiring isn't it?

Personal development

Another challenge amid all this is to develop your own skills. No one is perfect. CEOs also need to develop and improve. This is surprisingly difficult. It is a bit like trying to get fit when you are in the middle of a title fight.

In a world where knowledge is a critical organizational asset, great emphasis is placed on personal development. Corporate universities, e-learning programmes, in-house training, personal learning networks, these are just a few of the learning options available to employees. But what is available for those higher up the organization? What about CEOs who want to hone their leadership skills, acquire a deeper self-knowledge or maybe just retain their edge both mentally and physically?

The higher up you are the harder it is to do personal development. For a start, who delivers it? When you get to the top of the organization the issues you are dealing with are much more around leadership style, personal effectiveness, interpersonal skills, such as empathy, communication, listening, impact, clarity, and this is feedback and coaching that is very hard to give to anyone who is more senior than you or who is a colleague.

Externally, executive education programmes and CEO forums are options. But many senior executives are too busy running teams and organizations to take the time out to attend.

Just a few years ago, news that a CEO or senior executive was using a coach would have raised eyebrows in the boardroom. Today, however, assigning an executive coach to improve a leaders' management performance and/or overcome their personal development deficiencies is a far more acceptable practice.

For senior executives, the attractions of employing a coach are obvious. There is no need to leave the office for a start – a major plus for time-strapped executives. Better still, the coach fits into the executive's timetable, and provides a tailor-made programme focused solely on the needs of the executive.

Then there is the important issue of trust and confidentiality. 'We have this idea of organizations as pyramids, so at the top there's only space for one person. Also there are tactical reasons in the following sense: careers are individualistic, people are just not prepared for or used to sharing power. People are not used to trusting someone,' reflects José-Luis Álvarez. Sad but true, yet trust underpins the coaching relationship. 'An executive coach provides a safe place. Who else can CEOs turn to? They are surrounded by senior managers who drink from the same water fountain,' says one coach.

I have three individuals, totally outside the company, whom I rely on to run ideas past. I find their impartial, often difficult advice an important safety valve.

Feeling good, doing good, having fun

All of this only makes sense if there's a point to it all – the job, your organization, your career – which goes beyond simply making money for yourself and your employer. That's why corporate social responsibility (CSR) is a key aspect of any approach to leading people. It is important on a number of levels, but it also allows people to have some fun.

You probably think it sounds a little trivial. I don't think so. I think what we are talking about is a fundamental driver for the most talented people working at the cutting edge today, and that includes the senior team.

When talent reaches a certain level it wants something more than a pay cheque as a reward; it wants to feel that it makes a difference. Feeling that you are making a contribution does a lot for one's well-being.

Says Gary Knell of Sesame Workshop: 'At the end of the day, you've got to have fun at this job. When this stops becoming something that you get up in the morning and are really enthusiastic about coming in to tackle every day, it's probably time to move on.'

Importantly, having fun increases productivity. It makes people work harder, faster, smarter. The reality is that firms that focus on fun are more productive. When companies show a commitment to something bigger than the profit motive, they build loyalty and show soul. Firms that focus on making fun a part of their culture build a better work–life balance, which in turn means healthier, more motivated employees. It is the same for CEOs, where CSR and philanthropy can provide a sense of purpose beyond hitting earnings targets.

To some this sounds superficial, but I'm not alone in my genuine belief that CSR is an important aspect of any company's activities. Many other CEOs share this view. It's not just about doing good though, it has to make sound business sense.

'You cannot be sustainable if you do not have the financial results which afford it. It is being socially responsible in terms of being perfectly con-scious of the social impact of your company, says,' Jacques Aigrain, CEO at Swiss Re. 'In our case, as we don't make goods, it's mainly an issue of making sure that we have the appropriate processes in place to ensure that we are not providing insurance services to activities which would not be viewed as socially responsible. So we have a sustainability committee which checks on the appropriate compatibilities of some activities.'

This is CSR that goes to the heart of the business. 'There is also a very clearly aligned interest on the climate issue, because climate change has a very direct influence on our business and economic model. We are very vocal and very involved in all matters relating to climate, and by symbiosis on matters of water and the sustainability of water supplies,' says Aigrain. 'It's not just because we think it's lovely charity-oriented talk, but because it's highly compatible and essential for our business model. So it means being very involved in the debate, sponsoring a number of research projects, participating in the awareness campaigns and being highly visible in building awareness of the macroeconomic challenge related to climate change.'

Different strokes for different folks

Ask CEOs how they factor in some downtime and you will get a bunch of different answers. One they will all tell you, though, is even if, and especially if, you are a global CEO, you still need to take some time out to unwind, both physically and mentally.

'Careers are very jerky. People make huge contributions at various points in their career and they have a lot of time off,' observes Carl Schramm of the Kaufmann Foundation, who is a voracious reader in his downtime. Carl continues, 'Winston Churchill is a classic example and he's a fantastic inspiration. He led by ideas and endured a period when people just would not talk to him. And he saw the world so clearly. He had the courage of his convictions.'

One CEO told me about visiting another corporation where busyness reigned supreme. 'Every day there were two or three firm-wide new initiatives. Everybody had open calendars. The entire day, nine hours a day, was controlled by somebody else. People had to go to meetings but they didn't know what they were about. People were bombarded with ideas that weren't screened. If you wanted to manage your career up, you had to invest three or four hours a day just catching up with the news in the company. You can't manage a company like that. You overload.'

Jacques Aigrain, CEO of Swiss Re, is a strong believer in taking some 'thinking' time away from the everyday pressures of the job.

'Is it possible to switch off between work and home and home and work? I think it's critical. As the CEO you must take some distance from the day-to-day affairs and be able to focus on strategic matters, including people issues and the strategic direction of competitors, the market, yourself and your company. That means that there are moments when you will be utterly absorbed in issues which are a little more practical and short term.

'I'm lucky enough that 50 metres from my home I'm in the forest. I try to exercise every day and that's usually my best time for thinking, refreshing and finding a new angle on issues that I'm trying to deal with. That quality time, even though it's a limited number of hours with your husband or wife (or partner), with your kids, is also absolutely essential for finding the right balance.

'Because one of the results of being "wired" all the time is that you end up being disconnected from the real world.'

Key points

> Ultimately as the CEO of an organization, despite all the pressures of the job and its undoubted importance in terms of the organization, it is essential to retain a healthy perspective on work–life balance. CEOs should remember that they are in a privileged position. It may seem that so many people want a piece of them that there is nothing left to give – but there is always a little bit extra.

> Getting the balance right demands that the CEO travels when needed by the business, and travels healthily. It also requires that the CEO maximizes support networks and develops new skills as their career develops.

Resources

Álvarez, José Luis and Svejenova, Silviya, *Sharing Executive Power*, Cambridge University Press, 2005.

Bennett, Nathan and Miles, Stephen A., *Riding Shotgun: The Role of the COO*, Stanford Business Books, 2006.

Crainer, Stuart and Dearlove, Des, *Financial Times Guide to Business Travel*, Financial Times/Pearson Education, September 2001.

Fast Company/Roper Starch Worldwide, 'How much is enough?', *Fast Company*, June 1999, p.108.

Goldsmith, Marshall (with Mark Reiter), *What Got You Here Won't Get You There*, Hyperion, 2007.

National Sleep Foundation, *Less Fun, Less Sleep, More Work: An American Portrait*, NSF, 27 March 2001.

The CEO Report, FTdynamo, 2001.

Worrall, Les and Cooper, Cary L., 'Working patterns and working hours: their impact on UK managers', *Leadership and Organization Development Journal*, 20 (1999): 6–10.

Chapter **8**

Trials, tribulations and triumphs

What are the good things about the job? What are the worst?

While I am thinking about the company's long-term direction, it is vital for me to remain in touch with the current reality.

Carlos Ghosn, President and CEO, Nissan and Renault

Only validate

After talking with CEOs about their leadership theories and approaches I wanted to look at the day-to-day and find out the issues which really dogged them, the irritations, the worries and the pleasures.

'A good day for me is when I see healthy conflict inside the company,' Carlos Ghosn confided. 'People are confronting problems and tackling ways to solve them. They are working across departments and across functions to seek solutions or bring innovative ideas to the table. The solutions to all problems can be found inside the company, and I am encouraged when I see Nissan teams worldwide leveraging all the resources and talent available to them to create value. This gives me an indication that people are learning and the company is in a healthy state.'

'The best bit of the job is undoubtedly the fact that you suddenly realize, although maybe not in the first few months, that you can, surprisingly, truly influence a large, long-established organization,' says Jacques Aigrain, CEO of Swiss Re. 'You can see it change from a practical standpoint, from a people's behaviour standpoint, and from a dynamic and eventually a result standpoint, much faster than you would have imagined. It is quite wonderful, that you see that your efforts are not going to waste.'

Jacques Aigrain is right. CEOs change organizations and can shape people's behaviour, their expectations and their lives. Other CEOs took delight at more fundamental achievements. 'I am a recent CEO [eighteen months], but what I am most satisfied about is probably the mobilization of the whole organization on safety,' says Bruno Lafont, chairman and CEO of Lafarge. 'Safety is at the heart of our values, an organization like Lafarge must ensure the safety of its employees and contractors. Lafarge is already the best in its sector but we want to join best in class industrial companies. And I am deeply convinced that excellence in safety is leading to performance excellence overall. Each of our employees is now fully empowered in this effort, and this is something which has a strong value for our group.'

It is not all good, of course and it would be wrong to overlook the frustrating, depressing, and even downright bad bits that CEOs occasionally experience. 'I was never late, my whole life, until I got this job,' one CEO lamented in conversation. The job can break the habits of a lifetime. 'The thing I did wrong initially was watching the stock price too much,' another CEO confided.

'The less good part of the job would be the requirement to cajole and gently prod, again, again, and again, people at various levels of the organization, who tend to make changes or processes or adjustments or even business opportunities, more politically loaded than need be,' says Jacques Aigrain. 'You end up playing politics to help things get back. It's a waste of time.'

Truth be told, there are always going to be people in organizations who get in the way one way or another. The political nature of human beings is an occupational hazard for CEOs. 'Being busy doesn't bother me at all. The worst part of my job is individuals, and they're in every organization, who see a crystal-clear, calm pond and then throw a stone in it, just to see the ripples,' one CEO told me. 'It takes up time and disrupts the organization – some individuals, for whatever reason, think that's their reason in life. And usually the organization is two steps ahead of you in terms of who these people are. There are people saying, "Why don't you take this individual out?" And it is because there is always hope that you can change them, until you get to the point where you know they have to go.'

Changed perceptions

The reality is that when you become CEO relationships and expectations change. Seung-Yu Kim, CEO of Korea's Hana Financial Group, told me a very moving story about a close friend of his. They had graduated from high school together and their families knew each other. 'We were hand and glove,' Seung-Yu Kim remembers.

Seung-Yu Kim's friend's family ran a business manufacturing school uniforms. After graduation his friend succeeded his father to run the company. Then the Korean government suddenly changed the law on the wearing of school uniforms. The business needed to change and began looking at manufacturing fashionable clothing.

Seung-Yu Kim, with his corporate experience, realized that such a change of business was risky and counselled against it. Manufacturing school uniforms and fashionable clothing required different know-how and distribution channels, among other things. He tried to dissuade his friend but he did not listen.

Soon after, sales fell and the company's cash flow dried up. Seung-Yu Kim takes up the story: 'Finally he came to me, asking for some short-term operating capital. Based on my judgement, I had to refuse his request. There was no guarantee that his business would recover even if I provided some credit as a stopgap. My friend desperately asked for my help, relying on our long-time friendship, and he was enraged at my refusal. After a few weeks, I heard that his company was insolvent and eventually he was imprisoned. Afterwards, I asked myself hundreds of times why I had to choose this profession which caused me and my best friend to leave each other like that.'

A few years later, Seung-Yu Kim received a call from one of the local Hana Bank branch managers. He said that a friend of Seung-Yu Kim's had visited the branch and asked him to deliver an invitation to the wedding of the friend's daughter. Seung-Yu Kim recalls: 'It was him, the friend who had to go to prison because I refused to help him. I cancelled everything in my schedule and rushed down.

'There, I found my friend standing at his daughter's wedding to welcome guests. I knew I owed him an apology but he was the first one to talk. Grabbing my hands, he said, "Now I understand. Maybe I would have made the same choice as you had if I had been in your position." I couldn't say anything. We just hugged each other.

'I know I was lucky to recover my relationship with the friend after all. But the feelings I had to go through were the worst though they are commonly shared by those in the financial industry.'

Lemonade?

Talking to CEOs I found that the biggest day-to-day challenge and irritant was rewarding people. This was brought home to me on a family holiday. Every summer we go to North Carolina. Sitting on the front porch after a day at the beach my daughter and various of her friends thought it would be fun to make some lemonade and then set up a stand selling it at the front of the garden. The team was galvanized. Lemonade was made, a table dragged out, marketing materials created (by crayon), and the cash began to pour in. At 50 cents per lemonade it was attractively priced for the parched holiday makers on their way back from the beach. The kids all stood round excitedly as the first few customers parted with their money. We sat back with parental pride at their business acumen and enthusiasm.

Five minutes later, a few of the kids had drifted off. The marketing team were now chasing a butterfly. The pricing strategist was playing in the sand and others were dispersed around the garden doing what kids do. My daughter carried on gamely selling lemonade.

A couple of hours later the lemonade was exhausted and the money was added up: $12. My daughter asked everyone who had helped to stand in line to be paid. Everyone suddenly materialized. The marketers gave up on their butterfly, the pricing strategist abandoned the sand, and the garden looked a whole lot less interesting. They stood in line and held out their hands.

And that is how we are in organizations. We stand in line and hold out our hands for our bonuses. And if we don't get our share we kick up a fuss, even if we have been off with the butterflies.

This was brought home to me when I met up with a friend who works for a leading investment bank. Now, they know a thing or two about bonuses, but the same principles applied. He told me that a guy who got a $19 million bonus – he must have sold a lot of lemonade – was unhappy because he didn't get $19.2 million. Seriously. Why not $20 million, or $21? Why the 0.2?

People holding their hands out is a big issue for CEOs. Around 30 per cent of people move job because they want to be paid more. This group takes up a lot of CEO time.

It is an issue I have tried to manage myself. Early on in my time at Heidrick & Struggles I sent this email to all our staff:

Hi Everyone,

I like Fridays for two reasons:

1. The weekend is here and we can celebrate a great week

or

2. The weekend is here and we can say goodbye to a bad week

Personally, I have had a great week and learned a lot. I spent the first 3 days in Moscow, a fantastic city if you have a chance to visit, full of opportunity (and we have a very strong team there). While in Moscow I met a number of CEOs but one particular meeting sticks in my mind: it was with the CEO of a leading global bank.

The day of our meeting happened to be bonus day for this bank and he was a little on edge. We talked about how he was feeling and in particular the build-up of the past 6–8 weeks. He spoke about the need to 'manage expectations', wondering about retention issues and whether individuals would walk.

His firm had been acquired by this big global bank so it was not about him; it was about his genuine concern for his people. He told me: 'When I owned my firm, bonuses were decided on Wednesday and paid the following Monday, the wait is what kills you – compensation is so emotive and people stir each other up, endlessly predicting what might or might not happen.'

'It's amazing to watch', he said, 'because you get to a point where people can't separate fact from fiction – I am glad this will soon be over.'

The point of me sharing this with you is that we are approximately 5 weeks away from paying bonuses. And guess what? This year, like most others will be emotional – maybe even more so because of the changes we have made:

> ➤ *Moving to a single payment*
> ➤ *Overhauling the comp system*
> ➤ *Working to reunify the firm*

Change is something we all talk about but none of us seem too good at – and in times of change individuals always seem to think the worst.

So how can we make things better? Well, we all have choices, as individuals we can choose to thrive on the angst of the compensation roller coaster for the next few weeks OR we can recognize as an organization that the leadership of the firm wants to take care of its people – and will endeavor to do so.

Now, will there be individuals who we think will be happy that will be unhappy?

Absolutely.

Will there be individuals who we think will be unhappy that will be happy?

Absolutely.

In our firm of over 1,685 people will we make a few mistakes?

Absolutely.

And in this way we are no different from most organizations.

I promise we will do the best we can possibly do to recognize all those people who have contributed to the organization. It already looks like we've had a great start to the year: the global market is buoyant and I expect us to build on our successes in January month by month.

So, for those of you who had a great week . . . go celebrate. For those of you who had a bad week, go celebrate the fact that the week is over. Either way have a great weekend.

Kevin

Clock watching

The other big issue CEOs bring up repeatedly is time. As we have seen, for CEOs and many others in today's organizations, time is at a premium. Your days are mapped out for you with barely a few minutes' leeway. And then a colleague approaches you and whispers, 'Can I have five minutes?' Of course, you want to give them time. That is why you are there. You want to listen and talk. You want their ideas. You want to hear their worries and hopes.

But, the reality is that five minutes is never five minutes. It is usually thirty minutes, often an hour. Multiply those five minutes by the number of employees around the world and not much time remains in your career – let alone the working week.

CEOs all have a different approach to this. What unifies them is a sense that time is like gold dust. It had better be well used.

One CEO with even more pressures than normal is Carlos Ghosn, responsible for Nissan and Renault. 'I would say there are two ways I operate,' he explained to me. 'One is at a very high level. Being a CEO of two companies, I have learnt to empower based on a clear, unique, shared strategy. I screen decisions. If an executive can solve the problem, let him or her solve the problem. Coming to the CEO would be a waste of time. The principle of empowerment allows that only the toughest problems and the toughest decisions come to the CEO. Enabling decisions to be taken at the lowest level possible in the company can increase speed and gain precision.

'On another level, I want to remain in touch with reality. I spend as much time as I can to go visit the *gemba* – the people on the shopfloors – to listen to their opinions and see if there is anything that can be improved and implemented at the company level. This interaction allows me to stay in tune with what is going on in the company. People know that when I visit, I am there not for protocol, but to spend time with them, to hear their opinions and feelings, to praise them for their achievements and to encourage them in their challenges. When I go there, I fully engage myself with the team. Doing this allows me to keep myself focused on what is real.'

Richard Baker of Alliance Boots has developed his own unique approach. He is very disciplined and doesn't allow meetings to run over. 'I have found a good rhythm which works for me. You have to be ruthlessly well organized. I rarely cancel a meeting. I remember being a middle manager and people above changing their diaries. I am very punctual. If the CEO is disorganized there is a knock-on effect. If I was highly flexible or not punctual it would be chaos,' he says.

Another thing Richard does is to make deliveries with one of his company's trucks. It is amazing how many ways CEOs manage to spend time with their people and their customers. When he has a couple of hours that are free, Chip McClure instructs his assistant to block time out so he can walk around the company's technology centre, among other parts of the company. 'I just walk through, stick my head into an engineer's cubicle, and ask them what they're doing,' he says. 'The excitement and enthusiasm that I get from listening to our engineers is really infectious. I show up at the strangest times. I'll also go out to our garage. We've got an experimental garage where we do a lot of work for our customers. And I'll go out and spend time with our techs. As a matter of fact I was just out there a couple of weeks ago and three of them got their commercial drivers' licence, and we had a small cake-and-coffee celebration for them. Recognition, no matter how small, goes a long way, and that is important to me. My wife can tell when I've either been to a plant or in one of our engineering centres, because I'll come home with a different level of enthusiasm. It's this kind of excitement that tells me, hey, this is the future of the company. We've got some young, bright engineers and it's amazing to see the kind of things they can do?'

Listening intently

Another thing you commonly hear – though usually not directly – is that you don't listen to people's gripes. I was reminded of this when I spoke with H. Patrick Swygert. He told me about the extraordinary experience of meeting Nelson Mandela. 'When I met him two things were obvious to me. One, he appeared to be listening to what I had to say. Now, he's sitting in a chair, and the Nobel Peace Prize is right above his head on a wall, and I'm talking to Nelson Mandela, and it appeared as if he was actually listening to what I had to say. So I was incredibly flattered. And then secondly, in his response, it was clear he had listened to what I had to say, and I said to myself, well I'll follow this guy anywhere. He is giving me the benefit of listening to me, and digesting what I say. What a compliment! A worldwide figure, a charismatic personality, who doesn't need to hear what I have to say, but he's clever and empathetic enough, and enough of a leader, to both listen and to let me know he's listening. And then he began to talk about his vision for a free South Africa, in very simple declaratory sentences, it was obvious that he meant what he said and he said it well. So now he's listened to me, and he's told me something about where he'd like to go. Well, I want to be next to this guy, I don't want to leave him, and I think that's something that some people have, and some people do not.'

Nelson Mandela can listen, but his greatness and that of other leaders does not simply lie in listening; it lies in listening, giving your own opinion and then taking action. People may complain that you, as CEO, don't listen, but the reality is that you do listen, and then you make a decision, and if the decision is not what they want or have advised they accuse you of not listening. This point was brought home to me when I heard Tony Blair observe that 'The hardest thing about leadership is learning to ignore the loudest voices.'

Who is everyone?

Another frequently heard warning sign for the CEO is being told that 'Everyone thinks this', or 'That's what everyone is saying.' You need to constantly pin down who this *everyone* is. They are often mythical.

On this point, I frequently tell a story about four people named Everybody, Somebody, Anybody and Nobody.

There was an important job to be done and Everybody was asked to do it. Everybody was sure Somebody would do it. Anybody could have done it, but Nobody did it.

Somebody got angry about that, because it was Everybody's job. Everybody thought Anybody could do it but Nobody realized that Everybody wouldn't do it.

It ended up that Everybody blamed Somebody when Nobody did what Anybody could have done.

Any manager running any organization will recognize this story.

It really is about people

For me, the triumphs of the job are always connected to people – for example, a consultant in Europe ringing me up when I had taken over running his area and saying: 'This is the first time in ten years that I have been proud to be a member of this firm.'

Time and time again CEOs told me that the best thing about their job is the people. They're spot on. It is those moments when either you see people grow or do something great – get a big bit of business, get a big pitch – or someone you've hired gets promoted and is doing really well.

'I think a good manager is a mentor to all his people. Now, it can be dicey if your mentor is someone other than the person to whom you report. Reporting to Manager A and being mentored by Manager B requires good communication and trust,' says Gerry Roche of Heidrick & Struggles.

Key points

> Being a CEO is different. People see you differently and their expectations of you change.

> Top of the complaints league for CEOs are matters of rewards and remuneration. How the CEO approaches these issues and actively manages them is key to success.

> And then there is the lack of time. The only hope of managing your time is to hire a great assistant, manage meetings ruthlessly and refuse to be blindsided by requests for a quick five-minute discussion.

> The paradox is that though you have to ration your time rigorously, you have to spend a lot of time listening. None of this time is ever wasted – even if you choose to eventually ignore what you have heard.

> In the final analysis, successful CEOs are great at managing people. This is the job.

Chapter **9**

....

Tomorrow's CEOs

What is the identikit of the CEO of 2020? What skills and capabilities do you need to develop if you are to make the golden career leap?

What advice would you give somebody who aspired to be a CEO in the future? It would be to have conviction. You need passion and conviction, but also to be ready to adjust it for the human dimension. You may have a design, but you will have to play with the hand of cards that you have – your people.

Jacques Aigrain, CEO, Swiss Re

Chief entrepreneurial officers

The Kauffman Foundation develops innovative ideas to promote entrepreneurship and has, over four decades, become one of the largest foundations in the United States, with assets of approximately $2 billion. President and CEO of the Foundation, Carl J. Schramm, trained as an economist and lawyer and, for a time, worked in academia. His career evolved as he took on leadership roles with companies in the healthcare and insurance industries. An entrepreneur in his own right, Schramm was involved in numerous start-up ventures before being chosen as the CEO of Kauffman. The foundation, based in Kansas City, Missouri, was created by Ewing Kauffman, who went from salesman to founder of a pharmaceutical company which started in the basement of his home.

Schramm paints a powerful picture of the world that CEOs will have to manage tomorrow and the skills they will need as a result. 'Seventy per cent of college kids want to work for themselves. That's fantastic. When I got out of college you'd have four jobs between 22 and 65. I've got a son coming out of college next year. He's 22 and he'll have four jobs by the time he's 30. The chances are very high he'll work for himself in one of those four, or work with somebody he knows in college. And by the time he's 40 he will have had ten jobs.'

So, Schramm predicts a more freewheeling entrepreneurial environment. 'Some people are hedgehogs and some people are foxes. Foxes are innovators; hedgehogs, oddly I think, are entrepreneurs. People see entrepreneurs with lightning bolts going through their heads all the time, but I don't think that's right at all. I think the job of the entrepreneur is to take one good idea, settle it down, make the matrix work and deliver the product. A lot of our CEOs grow up in cultures in large corporations where they talk about entrepreneurship, but still hunt these entrepreneurs down and knock them off, because they are disturbing inside companies.'

The loyalty question

The need for more freewheeling entrepreneurial leaders is happening already. It is happening because the nature of our relationship with our employers has changed. Takeshi Niinami, CEO of Lawson in Japan, reflects that, of his intake of 200 into Mitsubishi, 160 still work with Mitsubishi or Mitsubishi subsidiaries. 'Loyalty is the real issue for Mitsubishi, for big companies. The younger generation want to challenge at an early stage.

They don't want to wait until they are 42 or 43 to become a general manager. For example, at Mitsubishi, if you want to be an executive they say you have to wait until age 54. Before then a lot of people get out and take opportunities to make themselves more capable in the market.'

The challenge for organizations now is that the next generation of senior executives may be motivated by factors other than the benefits package. Not only will they be seeking better work–life balance and more career flexibility, but they are likely to be looking just as hard for the opportunity and space to express their individuality as well. Now, that is a challenge.

Tomorrow's CEOs will be a whole lot more demanding of themselves and of their organizations. Carl Schramm again: 'Every single kid implicitly is brand managing himself. They're making a calculation every single day about the brand equity that they're building today. They're going to stay at IBM just as long as IBM continues to contribute to their brand equity, because that's their brand security. This is a real challenge for businesses in the future. The days of Michael Porter and the Strategic Retreat in November at a golf course with people from McKinsey telling you what the future of your company is, are over. The 25-year-olds from the engineering school have to be part of the whole dream.'

And the conclusion? Simple, says Carl: 'There's only one issue of the future – managing people.'

Tomorrow's CEOs

To better understand this new generation, I looked at research into high flying CEOs by London's Cass Business School and business writer Steve Coomber. This revealed a startling disparity in the ages of high performing CEOs across the globe. It also highlighted the executive stars of the future, listing the top fifty global high flying CEOs under the age of 45.

The study, which looked at the 52-week return on share prices of over 1,500 companies listed on the world's major stock exchanges, relies on efficient market theory, which states that, in a perfect world, in a perfect market, the share price of a company should reflect all information known about that company. Movements in share prices were used as an indicator of what the markets thought about particular companies, and therefore the CEOs.

Rather than compare companies in different regions directly, the returns were adjusted to account for local market movements by considering how a particular stock had outperformed the local market. The top performers were those CEOs who managed to outperform their local market by an impressive margin.

The first surprise in the research results is the lack of young CEOs in the United States. There was no CEO under 40 in the S&P 500. Across the world, the average age of a CEO was 54, and the most common age 57. This echoes the findings of past corporate surveys. In 1995, a Booz Allen Hamilton survey of the 2,500 largest publicly traded corporations revealed the average starting age of a CEO to be just over 50.

The youngest CEO in the survey was 29-year-old Sahba Abedian of Sunland, the Australian property group, the only CEO under 30. A further five were under 35, and nineteen more under 40. Although there were only twenty-five CEOs under 40, it was not all bad news for executives planning a swift route to the top.

Perhaps the most interesting results are those showing the rise of a cadre of young CEOs in China. Eight of the top ten CEOs in the ranking, and fourteen of the top twenty, lead companies listed in China. Nearly half (twenty-three) of the top fifty CEOs under the age of 45 are from China. The youngest is 33, and twelve are 40 or younger.

The Chinese CEOs head up some of the global corporate giants of the future. The top-ranked CEO on the list, Bin Zhao (aged 34) runs Shanghai Aero Auto Electromechanical (SAAE). The company gets over 80 per cent of its revenue from auto parts and is also involved in satellite development. Turnover for 2005 was CNY 1.8 billion ($225.7 million), while net profit guidance for the first half of 2006 was up 300 per cent on 2005 at CNY 13.2 million ($1.6 million).

'The old argument is that age brings experience and wisdom, qualities that help produce good performance,' says Neil Beasley, the Cass MBA student who conducted the research. 'If true, you would expect to see a link between older people performing better than younger people. Almost across the board that link wasn't present. If they have got the skills, and they are in the right place at the right time, younger CEOs can perform just as well as those with ten or twenty years' more experience.'

To sum up all of this I spoke to my colleague Steve Tappin. 'I believe that the next generation of CEOs are going to be more like corporate entrepreneurs,' said Steve. 'They'll have worked and managed, been MDs of significant businesses, that will be international in nature, that will have complexity, and at the same time, they'll have spent some periods in a young, high growth businesses as well, and may have spent some time in start-ups and private equity. So I think the new generation of CEOs won't come from the traditional career path, I think that's over – Oxford, ICI, BP, MBA. I think there'll be a lot more people who have switched, and have had different experiences.'

Greater diversity

Current CEOs are already detecting the winds of change. There is no question that the CEO of the future is likely to be younger, more entrepreneurial, more aware of their own brand, and more likely to reflect the increased diversity of globalization.

I asked Bruno Lafont, chairman and CEO of Lafarge, what qualities he thought the CEO of the future would need to succeed. 'I think he/she will need to have an even stronger international experience, in particular it will probably be key that he/she has been exposed to Asia during his or her career. He or she will need to have a strong leadership and to be an excellent communicator, in order to clarify the vision and the strategy as much as possible, in a world that is getting more and more complex. I think he or she will be closer to people and to the business on the ground than CEOs could be in the past, because everything is becoming more global but also much more local.'

'Logically there may be more Chinese and Indian and fewer American CEOs; that's a pure characteristic of world economic changes,' says Jacques Aigrain, CEO of Swiss Re. 'In a recent visit to our office in Beijing, seeing the level of enthusiasm and quality of the young Chinese that we have in the office, the challenge and opportunity is that in twenty years' time maybe the CEO of Swiss Re should be one of them. It would be the logical development. So that's thinking truly globally and truly about the evolution of our world as something that's become very small and unified.'

I asked Nissan's Carlos Ghosn what he considered the skills demands on CEOs of the future. His response begins with a sense of responsibility for your actions: 'You cannot lead people in the twenty-first century if somehow you do not assume the consequence of your actions. And the consequence of your actions cannot be simply saying, "I made a mistake." No. From time to time you have a vision, you have a plan, you have a strategy, you have an objective. You are asking people to work day and night for them, and you have to assume that personally. That is the management of the twenty-first century.

'The priority of a company president is to be where the toughest problems or the toughest fronts are. He or she has to be someone who clarifies and takes the most difficult decisions. Then make sure they are in the most risky places, showing up and supporting people on the front lines.

'Another increasingly important skill needed in this century is the ability to create value and strength out of diversity, not out of coherence and uniformity. The identity of the corporation is global. You need to know how people from different continents, cultures and experiences can work in a very effective way to provide something meaningful and to compete against much more coherent organizations that are monocultural. If you can manage this, you will create a definite competitive advantage because diversity always brings more innovative ideas and wealth to the company even though it is harder to manage.'

Talent spotting

A decade ago three McKinsey consultants famously declared a war for talent. I was in Asia recently when a CEO stood up at dinner and said: 'Good news, the war for talent is over. Talent won.'

I believe there is a new war: the war to serve that talent. What is clear today is that talent is creating new markets. Whether its hedge funds, private equity, technology, or creative industries, these are microeconomies dreamt up by the sheer power of imagination. From new markets in the geographies of eastern Europe to the fledgling economies of Asia, talent is spawning new ideas and new concepts. Recently at Heidrick & Struggles we have picked up a CIO (chief intellectual officer) search, a CSO (chief security officer) and a CSR (chief social responsibility officer). All brand new roles dictated by the needs of today's talent on a swiftly tilting planet. Half of these jobs didn't exist five years ago.

What will happen by the time our children hit the workforce? There is some evidence to suggest that people from generation Y/generation iPod, or whatever digital epithet they are labelled with, are looking for something more than money. Better work–life balance and more career flexibility for a start, and, judging by their MySpace and Facebook pages, the ability to express their individuality – surely a challenge for any organization.

At the other end of the spectrum the population is ageing. Over the next twenty-five years there will be 75 million fewer Europeans, 65 million fewer Japanese. What does all this tell us? Simply that tomorrow will be different – as different as 1980 was from today, if not more so. Tomorrow is going to be as different as today's talent can imagine it to be.

This all leaves the CEO of the future in a more complicated role than ever before. 'The days of the iron-fisted, iron-willed outsized personality CEO are gone. Those individuals have gone the way of the dinosaurs,' says H. Patrick Swygert of Howard University. 'For the CEO of the future it's going to take incredible flexibility. Governance is going to be so radically different five years from now, not just ten or fifteen or twenty. It's going to take an agile CEO to wade through internal and external governance issues, deal with globalization and regulation while keeping a strategic eye out for opportunities and challenges for the business. I think it's going to be an increasingly challenging position.' In truth, it always was, but the challenges just got bigger.

Key points

> The CEOs of tomorrow will be younger. They will be more entrepreneurial and their loyalty will be to themselves and their own brand – Brand You as the business guru Tom Peters puts it.

> They will embrace diversity and have to get used to incredible levels of complexity.

> Finding such talented individuals will become an ever more pressing issue in the world's boardrooms.

Resources

Beasley, Neil, Coomber, Steve, 'The top 50 up and coming CEOs', *CEO Magazine*, September 2006.

Lucier, Chuck, Wheeler, Steven and Hobbel, Rolf, 'CEO Succession 2006: the era of the inclusive leader', Booz Allen's annual CEO succession study, *Strategy+Business*, Summer 2007.

Michaels, Ed, Handfield-Jones, Helen and Axelrod, Beth, *The War for Talent*, Harvard Business School Press, 2001.

Wooldridge, Adrian, 'The battle for brainpower', *The Economist*, 5 October 2006.

Chapter **10**

....

The life beyond

Nothing lasts for ever. Today's magazine-cover CEO superstar is tomorrow's corporate footnote. But how does this affect CEOs when they're in the job and how can they prepare for the life beyond?

It is a tough job. It's better in the rear view mirror. Like climbing a mountain, it's not enjoyable every minute. You are endlessly overcoming problems, but it's great when you reach the summit.

Richard Baker, CEO, Alliance Boots

Tough going

No one ever said it was going to be easy. Indeed, when the going gets tough is when the CEO really earns his or her spurs. Ask Carlos Ghosn: 'As a CEO, your performance cannot be judged merely when the company is successful and in good shape. This is not meaningful. No, your performance should also be judged by what you demonstrate when you are in a hole, when you are in trouble. Then you are going to be tested on your values. What are the things you believe in? What you are going to give away? What will you stand for even if more sacrifices are required? This is the real demonstration of the things you believe in.'

I absolutely agree with this. I have an unidentified quote pinned to my office noticeboard which reminds me of what Carlos Ghosn is talking about. It says, 'At decisive moments leadership is about moving against the stream, asking yourself not what the peope want right now, but rather what the people need in the long term and what should be done about it now. It's not easy; leadership has its risks. But when leaders aren't ready to lead, many other people have to pay the price.'

Ghosn continues: 'In Nissan in 1999 and 2000, what we stood for was obvious. We eliminated everything we did not stand for, and we kept everything we believed in. In a certain way, the results we are getting today and will get in the future can be considered the reward or punishment for what we have done or did not do.

'The challenge is in motivating people when you are going to restructure the company, close plants, reduce headcounts, dismantle keiretsu, dismantle cross-shareholding. You can understand the contradiction and why a lot of people cannot go through the process of change easily. Sometimes people go brutally into what they have to do, neglecting others' motivation, and they end up with a disaster. For example, cost reduction can build up a company if it is motivating, if it is within a purpose, if it points people towards an attractive destination and if they understand the reason why they have to go through a difficult period. But if nobody invests in them to show them the purpose and if they do not have the impression that they own the process, then cost reduction can be extremely destructive. This was one of our most challenging experiences in reviving Nissan.'

Sell-by dates

Tough times need to be faced, and faced with the sure knowledge that any crisis might be your last. Nothing lasts for ever – though sometimes it feels as if it might. Sidney Harman, who runs Harman International Industries, is 85 years old and still going strong. The head of Viacom is almost that age. In the past year or so, several older CEOs have been pressed back into service. Gerry Grinstein was brought in at Delta at the age of 71. John Reed was no kid when he went to the New York Stock Exchange.

Perhaps more galling than being out of a job is that when you leave you might just have set up the next guy to succeed. Look at Carly Fiorina. Hewlett-Packard is now enthusiastically reaping the benefits of her strategy.

Even so, CEOs are surprisingly honest about how long they are likely to stay in the job. They are realistic almost to a fault.

Monika Ribar of Panalpina told me, 'I am absolutely convinced that I am for the time being the absolute right person for this job here. But I'm not sure if I will still be in five years. You see, the company is always changing. Normally, when we have to replace somebody, for whatever reason, and let's say the predecessor has done a good job, we tend just to look for a copy of the predecessor – which is not necessarily the best person for the time being and especially for the next five years. Our company really needed strong leadership and clear targets because that was missing in the past, but in five years' time the company might need a much more sales-oriented person than I am.'

They are honest because they see themselves as stewards of the organization. The organization is bigger than they are. Once this balance is out of kilter – when the CEO's ego takes over – you begin to have problems.

Time and time again, the CEOs I spoke to talked of stewardship and of what they would leave behind, their legacy. Typical of their sentiments were those of Gary Knell: 'You've got to keep long-term stewardship in mind. What I try to do is project how I would feel if I was not the CEO but I was on the board. What would I ask the CEO? What objective criteria would I use to evaluate his or her performance? I think by putting yourself in their position you can have a more objective mirror on your own performance and whether you're really making a positive impact on the organization and maximizing your potential as an executive. I think that's a really important thing to do.

The reality is you're only going to be able to lead less than a handful of important changes at the end of the day – directional changes of the company, maybe it's about a new line of business or maybe it's a new part of the world that you've engaged in – but there's not going to be more than five, and I think you're going to find it's going to be two or three things that people will remember you by, even if you do a great job. So, I think keeping that in mind is really important. It's about remembering that long-term stewardship is about moving an organization and leaving a legacy of change that will in the long run really help the organization to prepare itself for the next generation of leadership.'

Your legacy

Seung-Yu Kim of Hana Financial Group also thinks of himself as a temporary steward of the company. 'This is your company, not my company,' he tells employees. 'My tenure is only three years and the shareholders decide whether they are going to re-elect me. But your tenure is 58 years, so it is your company, not mine.'

Takeshi Niinami, CEO of Lawson, told me that part of his job was to understand the company's history. This was something he worked at. 'I learnt about the history of Lawson in detail, from reading reports and also listening to people who had retired and who were going to retire. The company history is important, because that's the legacy. By understanding the history it also helps you prepare for the future.'

The future is always on the CEO's mind. 'CEOs have to see the future, they can't celebrate together with other executives when things go well today,' lamented one CEO. Where is the company going? What does the CEO want to leave behind? 'I think my vision is that after my departure, maybe five or six or even three years after, people will see my role as great. Because what I left is the people, that's why the company can enjoy, a legacy of great people,' says Takeshi Niinami.

What got you here might not get you there

While CEOs need to have a constant eye on their legacy, they must also be aware that their own skills need to change. It is not simply impatient investors or unpredictable markets which spell the end for CEOs. In many companies, ambitious executives walk a knife's edge between the healthy drive to get on and destructive behaviours that can ruin their careers.

The Center for Creative Leadership in Greensboro, North Carolina, has been researching career derailment since 1983. Its findings suggest that, each year, as many as half of all high flying executive careers derail – the executive gets fired, is demoted or reaches a career plateau. Typically, these are people who have been placed on a fast trajectory for the top. Two of the main derailment factors are the inability or unwillingness to change or adapt; and problems with interpersonal relationships.

Other studies have examined why some high flyers suddenly experience a catastrophic reversal in their career progress, in some cases accompanied by psychological trauma. They suggest that a manager's perceived strengths often contribute to their downfall. What appear to be positive characteristics early on in an individual's career can also have a dark side.

Succession planning

What is strange about the CEO's job is that you have an obligation to nurture a successor. The final element which should be in the CEO's job description is one of the most neglected: succession planning.

According to Warren Bennis and James O'Toole, getting CEO succession right requires boards to:

1 Come to a shared definition of leadership.

2 Resolve strategic and political conflicts.

3 Actively measure the soft qualities in CEO candidates.

4 Beware of CEO candidates who act like CEOs: they should avoid being seduced by charisma.

5 Recognize that real leaders are threatening: the safe choice may be the wrong choice.

6 Know that insider heirs usually aren't apparent: crown princes should be vetted with the same rigour as outsiders.

7 Don't rush to judgement.

'Part of good board governance is making good plans and identifying candidates for succession,' one CEO told me. 'I've been CEO for eleven years and that's long enough. It's a stressful job, but getting the board involved with the succession process is not an easy task either. First of all the CEO has got to get him or herself mentally prepared; but then you've got to engage your board in it.'

This particular CEO had spent four years on the succession process. 'We asked ourselves what the next CEO in this changing business environment should be like? What sorts of skills or competences should he or she have? Even though you know you're not going to get all of these competences in one candidate, nevertheless you should be able to identify what you want.

'We got into skills sets and we got into innate qualities that you can't train for. We talked about language skills – should the next CEO in a global society have multiple language capability? We talked about the global mindset and those sorts of things.'

As well as skills set, the process also identified some innate qualities that could not be trained, including leadership style. 'If you think about a leader who identifies with external or internal stakeholders, we wanted a CEO to have probably a little bit more external stakeholder focus than internal. We even talked about the spouses and their role in the organization. We thought we needed a corporate cheerleader in the organization, someone to meet the press and be constantly involved with big customers. That's all style of leadership – that's not education or basic skills sets', says the CEO.

Making a mark

As I was finishing this book, I had an opportunity to interview Stuart Rose, CEO of retailer Marks & Spencer. Rose's story made an interview irresistible. Talking to him it became clear that he embodied much of what I have talked about in this book; he might be seen as a true benchmark CEO. I punctuate his story of the revival of Marks & Spencer with the main points which it highlights.

It begins with luck and timing rather than career planning

After working for Marks & Spencer (M&S), Stuart Rose worked for the Burton Group, Argos, Booker and Arcadia. As his career had taken off, M&S's fortunes had declined. In May 2004 it was announced that M&S's chairman, Luc Vandevelde, was departing. Soon after, Stuart Rose had a Thursday morning meeting with non-executive director Kevin Lomax. A few hours later, the retailer Sir Philip Green launched a hostile takeover for M&S with £8 billion tabled as his offer. Later that evening, M&S approached Stuart Rose and by the following Monday he was installed as the company's CEO. Being in the right place at the right time is as important at the top of the corporate tree as it is anywhere else.

The first days count

Stuart Rose spent the first weeks and months of his leadership of M&S fighting off Philip Green's unwelcome takeover bid. It was not until July 2004 that the spectre of a takeover was averted. Having a clear short-term challenge helped focus energies.

If everything were perfect they wouldn't need a new CEO. The CEO usually encounters trouble

When Rose took over as CEO, the once legendary UK retailer was on its knees. To put its problems in perspective, in 1997 M&S was the second largest market capitalized retailer in the world after Wal-Mart; M&S was capitalized at $25 billion and Wal-Mart $60 billion. By 2005/6 M&S was capitalized as the 28th largest retailer, still at $25 billion (having been down to $12 billion), and Wal-Mart was at $300 billion. M&S was saddled with a mountain of inventory – £3 billion worth. Its clothing range was confusingly branded, with sixteen sub-brands. M&S was slow to move with fashion and its clothes looked increasingly dowdy in its cluttered high street stores. Among other problems, consultants were running thirty-one 'strategic projects.'

But the CEO may have nothing to lose

'Believe it or not, I don't think they saw me as a white knight; I think they saw me as absolute desperation: "Well we are not sure he can do it but he is the last resort, so let's give it a try." I'm not being falsely modest!' says Rose.

'Obviously, if you come into a business that is in a crisis you have the disadvantage that you're coming in at a crisis, but actually you have a bigger advantage – the advantage is that the board frankly would have agreed to anything. I had absolute control, which was key.

'The second thing is that I've been in a few businesses that have been in a bit of trouble in the last ten years or so and I think what I spotted fairly early on is that it wasn't as if they were careering away in the wrong direction, they just weren't doing anything at all.'

Take action to achieve momentum

The great thing about a crisis is that action is necessary immediately. There is no time to hatch a complex strategy and then to roll it out through the organization. A willingness to roll your sleeves up and execute is what the organization needs. Think back to Lou Gerstner's comments when he took over at IBM. Gerstner realized that the last thing IBM needed at that time was a vision; it needed to act. This was the case at M&S. It wasn't so much that the company was continuing to make the wrong decisions. It had made them and was standing amid the results without much idea of what to do next.

This situation was made for Stuart Rose. 'It's a bit like the old stories – people are so desperate for leadership even if you lead them the wrong way they'd rather go that way than go nowhere at all. People were almost literally standing around saying either, "There isn't a problem, what problem?"

Or, "There is a problem but we don't know what to do about it." Some were saying go left and some were saying go right; and the rest, well, it just passed over their heads.'

Straight talk from the start

If you take over a company in a muddle – or worse – there is little to be said for politeness and understatement. Talk straight and act in accordance with what you say. Think of our earlier discussion about communication.

At M&S, Rose set about restructuring the company, concentrating on making cost savings of some £260 million. Six hundred and fifty of the 3,500 corporate employees left. He felt it was important that his deeds matched his words from the very start. 'What I felt was that you had to talk the talk and say it as it was. And remember, we were fighting a bid at the time – so we needed to say it as it is, not only to the press whom we were trying to win over and get our point across to, but also internally. Because if you were saying it to the press you couldn't then not do something internally, so that again was an advantage because it gave me a double strength.'

Nearly right now is often better than perfection tomorrow

In a complex and difficult business situation with the press and expectant employees hanging on your every word, the chances of hatching a watertight, perfect strategy are extremely slim. You have to compromise on perfection to execute in accordance with what the company desperately needs. Stuart Rose remembers what he told himself: 'Be 95 per cent right rather than 100 per cent right; follow your gut instincts; cut back minimally on research; use the benefit of thirty years' experience; you aren't going to be right in every respect but mostly you could get it right by touch or feel, and then if you are in any doubt at all about doing something today or doing something tomorrow, do it today.' Of course, as Rose candidly admits, mistakes are made.

Not everyone signs up for change. You have to manage them

Rose identified three types of people at M&S. First, there were those who actually knew there was a problem and wanted to cure it. Second, there were those who could probably be persuaded to recognize there was a problem. Finally, there were those who refused to believe anything was wrong. Unfortunately, as is often the case, those in the third group tended to be the longer-serving people, the 'organization's glue'. The removal of a number of board members helped convince some of the people with doubts that Rose was serious and that their jobs were at risk.

Change and leadership begin with conversation

Bold decision making has to be backed by consistent and committed communication. Always. 'I sat down with probably twenty managers in the first week,' says Rose. 'I said, "Come in, sit down, you don't know me" – though one or two of them did remember me from my previous time with the company. I said, "Tell me what you think the problems are in the business. Tell me what you think we should do, tell me how you think we should fix it." There were those saying, "I'm so glad that somebody like you has come in. You're talking about products, you're talking about prices, you're talking about shopkeeping. You know, if only we could do this, this, this or this." So you put them down as a tick.

'There were others saying, "There's no problem here, absolutely alright, all you need to do is leave us to ourselves and go and do something else because my bit of the company's absolutely fine." And there were those who weren't quite sure what to do. Interestingly enough, they were the most difficult ones because you had to make a very quick decision as to whether you could get them there or was it just going to take you too long. Can you teach this person to swim before the pool fills up, or can't you?'

Communicate key positive messages repeatedly

Negativity is corrosive. To stand any chance in the job, a CEO has to quickly identify positive messages and continually emphasize them. Repetition of key messages is the hard graft of leadership.

Says Stuart Rose: 'We tried, often via some very simple things, to give people their confidence back because the morale of the business was very damaged. There was a feeling of inevitability about the fact that we were a mid-market retailer either going to be undermined by cheaper competitors, like Matalan and Primark, or be completely swamped by competitors with mass appeal like Tesco. We reminded people that this was not a new problem. We had had competition through the preceding 110 years of our history in different forms and different shapes and different places. This was just another manifestation of the same problem, but this time we just weren't dealing with it. So we used to go back and remind them what was the best things about Marks & Spencer? I still use that a lot. Quality, value, service, innovation and trust are the five words we always use, and the three most important things we need to do are to have better products, to have better shops and to have better service. I still use those five words almost every day in this business and I'm pretty certain now most people can remember them and say, actually he's got a point.

Easy wins

'We also had to find one or two places where we could demonstrate that there was traction. I've always said that womenswear is the key to the golden gate of Marks & Spencer. You want to get the key to the doors of happiness? You get that golden key that goes into womenswear. Menswear will come right, childrenswear will come right, lingerie will come right, everything will come right if you get womenswear right.

'But the other bit of the business which had kept up very well was food. Despite the fact that food revenues were down a little, we hadn't prostituted our values and had kept up our rate of innovation. So there was a dichotomy of customers. Women were coming in with their blinkers on walking through the clothing department to go downstairs to the food hall, thinking – "Oh, I won't look at the clothing because the clothing's all terrible."

'So, we had to work on womenswear first. I was lucky because, although I didn't hire her, Kate Bostock who now heads womenswear and lingerie had been retained a couple of months before I came. I said, "Your priority is to fix this. Forget about everything else, I'll worry about the shops."'

Challenging people to solve their own problems

Keeping up to date with fashion trends, Stuart Rose was leafing through *Vogue* when some shoes caught his eye. Next day, he went into the footwear department and asked why M&S didn't have similar style shoes in their range. On the next afternoon, the head of operations for footwear let Rose know that the shoes had now been designed and the factory in China was ready to begin production. The shoes arrived ten days later. 'I used him a lot as an example at the time,' says Rose. 'It was about showing people this is a problem we can solve. A couple of youngsters were suddenly starting to say, "Stuart, by the way I've done this." It was sort of exponential. One guy did something I made an example of, then another guy wants to see if he can do that, then a couple more. Steve Rowe in homewear is a very aggressive trader and he began slashing the prices. We used to sell a towel rail for £21 or £22; the same towel rails of the same quality are now £9.50. That's in the space of twenty-four months and we're selling tens of thousands.'

Delegate, but only so far

Stuart Rose reined in the company's appetite for delegating decision making down the management hierarchy. 'My predecessor believed in devolution of responsibility down the chain. I understand the principle but he did it willy nilly and that led to complete anarchy. Instead of being Marks & Spencer where everything was unified, what you had was shops called Marks & Spencer but everyone was running their own departments. It was a bit like a bazaar. There was the lingerie bazaar, there was the menswear bazaar, there was the womenswear bazaar, there was the food bazaar. Nobody was talking to each other. They all had their own marketing, they all had their own heads of this, their own heads of that, they had their personnel people, their marketing people. So I grabbed hold of that and said, "One controlled stock inventory. You can't spend the company's or stockholders' money without speaking to somebody in the centre, and he works for me now. You can't have your own ideas about handwriting or what Marks & Spencer's stands for," etc.

'It was about grabbing hold of the organization and filtering out: these jobs are done centrally, these jobs are devolved, you can't do that any more but you can do that. But within the bit you can do you've got total autonomy. So it was, it was setting those benchmarks and those frameworks.'

Manage complexity and ambiguity

Fending off an unwelcome bid and turning around an ailing company means that there is a lot going on at the sametime. This has to be managed. 'What actually happened was there was a heck of a lot of things all happening at once and you didn't have a clue what was going to come out at the end. It was a bit like cooking an omelette. We were throwing eggs in, throwing salt in, throwing this in, throwing that in, mixing it all up and sticking it in the pan hoping something decent would come out. I didn't know any other way.'

Manage the board

Of course, Rose is candid about the trials and tribulations along the way. There were troubled moments in the relationship between him and the board. In spring 2005 one of the non-executive directors pointed out that since Rose's arrival in the previous July the revenue line hadn't moved upwards. Rose retorted that he had actually said, in the full glare of publicity, that the revenue line would move downwards but the profit line would move upwards and the quality of earnings would improve. It was not until the autumn of 2005 that the top line started to improve.

Changing strategy in mid-stream is not an option

Sometimes companies and their leaders need to hold their breath and just jump. There can be no going back. Executing on a plan is often preferable to cogitating about potential new plans or changing the plan halfway down. 'There is no plan B,' confesses Rose. 'I remember telling the chairman in quite the same way about this, saying, "Well, look, if I can't fix the business don't ask me if I have an alternative plan. I haven't got one. I've only got one plan and we're just going to keep going at this, guys, until either I get sacked or I'm proved right. There ain't no turning, we're not moving left or right. That's the way, that's going to pay off and I won't change the plan now."'

Improving morale takes time

Change is rarely instant. 'We didn't really get an improvement, a significant improvement, in morale business-wide or even head-office-wide until the sales line started improving at the back end of 2005. People were still standing there saying, "Yes, I like that. He's saying the right thing but it's never going to work." Or, "Yes, nice idea." Or they'd get enthusiastic for a week and then the sales would come in the following Monday and they still wouldn't be very good so they'd go back to being unhappy. Retail is a bit like that – you know we are a sales-driven business.

'We're still not fully repaired because this is quite an intelligent and quite a cynical organization and, of course, we have been here before and we had a revival of some sort back at the beginning of the decade. People now keep saying, "Well, it happened before what's to stop it all going bad again?"'

Carry on raising the bar

M&S recorded a profit of £965 million in 2007. For Stuart Rose this was a marker for future improvement. 'If the speed of sound is 850 miles an hour we need to be doing 1,000 miles an hour by this time next year. That's a big test. And I can't look you in the eye and tell you I'm sure it's going to happen. But I know that if it doesn't happen it will be a real crisis for the business because in our heads we've got a three-year plan which is to take the business from £8 or £9 billion of turnover to £12 billion of turnover. I'm not interested in saying, how do I make it go from 8.5 to 9.1 or 9.1 to 9.6? I'm saying, how do we make this business go from an £8 billion corporation to a £12 billion corporation?'

Reward people for performance

M&S had previously rewarded people for the length of their service rather than their performance. A series of incentives and performance-related plans are now in place throughout the organization. Says Stuart Rose: 'Old Marks & Spencer would have said, blame the management. Now we say, blame yourself – if you didn't get a bonus, you didn't earn it. If your colleagues aren't getting a bonus, you let them down. Quite rightly, it goes right the way down the staff – to the girl on the till who has just been given a £500 bonus because she met her service levels to the store, because she gave the customer a smile, because she sold more volume, because the letters I get now all say that the service is so much better. And if 55,000 or 50 of our customer assistants do that every day we'll all get rich, and if they don't then we're stuffed.'

Like the CEO's job, it is as simple and as complex as that.

Key points

> The final ingredient is the future. Unlike virtually any other job, CEOs have to manage their own succession. Great companies have great succession planning and CEOs who have a constant eye on their own legacy to the organization.

> CEOs are never for ever. They are stewards of values, stewards of reputation and guardians of high performance.

Resources

Bennis, Warren and O'Toole, James, 'Don't hire the wrong CEO', *Harvard Business Review*, 78 (2000): 170–7.

Galford, Robert and Fazio, Maruca Regina, *Your Leadership Legacy*, Harvard Business School Press, 2006.

McCauley, Cynthia D., Moxley, Russ S. and Van Velsor, Ellen (eds), *The Center for Creative Leadership Handbook of Leadership Development*, Jossey-Bass, 1998.

Rothwell, William J., *Effective Succession Planning, Amacom*, 2005.

Sims, Doris, *Building Tomorrow's Talent*, Authorhouse, 2007.

Index